Scholars Praise
Śrī Īśopaniṣad

"The eighteen Sanskrit mantras of *Śrī Īśopaniṣad* are given in both *devanāgarī* and roman script, something that will be of great help to the beginning student. Swami Prabhupāda has given intelligent and lucid commentaries on every *mantra,* and—unusual for this type of publication—a glossary and index have been added."

Dr. Paul Hockings
Professor of Anthropology
University of Illinois

"The first available English edition of *Śrī Īśopaniṣad* makes this most significant publication accessible to a broader public of students and scholars. This spiritual law book, with a most useful introduction by His Divine Grace A.C. Bhaktivedanta Swami Prabhupāda, is a necessary supplement to any serious study of Vedic culture. The Sanskrit diacritical equivalents and the glossary are most useful guides to further study and deeper understanding of ancient spiritual law and Vedic culture.

"I recommend this volume to any student or scholar of Vedic thought. To the generalist and specialist alike it will generate considerable provocation and understanding. It is an indispensable addition to any serious library collection."

Dr. Thomas N. Pappas
Professor of History
[illegible]

श्री ईशोपनिषद्

Śrī Īśopaniṣad

BOOKS by His Divine Grace
A. C. Bhaktivedanta Swami Prabhupāda

Bhagavad-gītā As It Is
Śrīmad-Bhāgavatam (completed by disciples)
Śrī Caitanya-caritāmṛta
Kṛṣṇa, the Supreme Personality of Godhead
Teachings of Lord Caitanya
The Nectar of Devotion
The Nectar of Instruction
Śrī Īśopaniṣad
Light of the Bhāgavata
Easy Journey to Other Planets
Teachings of Lord Kapila, the Son of Devahūti
Teachings of Queen Kuntī
Message of Godhead
The Science of Self-Realization
The Perfection of Yoga
Beyond Birth and Death
On the Way to Kṛṣṇa
Rāja-vidyā: The King of Knowledge
Elevation to Kṛṣṇa Consciousness
Kṛṣṇa Consciousness: The Matchless Gift
Kṛṣṇa Consciousness: The Topmost Yoga System
Perfect Questions, Perfect Answers
Life Comes from Life
The Nārada-bhakti-sūtra (completed by disciples)
The Mukunda-mālā-stotra (completed by disciples)
Geetār-gān (Bengali)
Vairāgya-vidyā (Bengali)
Buddhi-yoga (Bengali)
Bhakti-ratna-boli (Bengali)
Back to Godhead magazine (founder)

BOOKS compiled from the teachings of His Divine Grace
A. C. Bhaktivedanta Swami Prabhupāda after his lifetime

Search for Liberation
Bhakti-yoga, the Art of Eternal Love
The Journey of Self-Discovery
Dharma, the Way of Transcendence
The Hare Kṛṣṇa Challenge
Renunciation Through Wisdom
A Second Chance
Beyond Illusion and Doubt
Civilization and Transcendence
Spiritual Yoga
The Laws of Nature
The Quest for Enlightenment

Śrī Īśopaniṣad

The Knowledge That Brings One Nearer to
The Supreme Personality of Godhead, Kṛṣṇa

With introduction, translation
and authorized purports by

His Divine Grace
A. C. Bhaktivedanta Swami
Prabhupāda

Founder-*Ācārya* of the International Society
for Krishna Consciousness

THE BHAKTIVEDANTA BOOK TRUST
LOS ANGELES • STOCKHOLM • MUMBAI • SYDNEY

THE COVER: Beauty, mystery and unlimited power unite in the form of the Lord, the *Īśa* in *Īśopaniṣad.* Here He is depicted as Śrī Keśava, one of the Viṣṇu expansions of Lord Kṛṣṇa, the Supreme Personality of Godhead.

Readers interested in the subject matter of this book are invited by the International Society for Krishna Consciousness to correspond with its Secretary at one of the following addresses:

International Society for Krishna Consciousness
P.O. Box 341445
Los Angeles, California 90034, USA
Telephone: 1-800-927-4152 (inside USA);
1-310-837-5283 (outside USA)
e-mail: bbt.usa@krishna.com • web: www.krishna.com

The Bhaktivedanta Book Trust
P.O. Box 380,
Riverstone, NSW 2765
Australia

Previous printings (1996–2016): 600,000
Current printing, 2021: 20,000

Third Edition

Printed in China

Library of Congress Cataloging-in-Publication Data

Upanishads. Īśopaniṣad. English.
Śrī Īśopaniṣad : the knowledge that brings one nearer to the supreme personality of Godhead, Kṛṣṇa ; with introduction, translation and authorized purports / by A. C. Bhaktivedanta Swami Prabhupāda.
p. cm.
Includes index.
ISBN 0-89213-138-1
I. A. C. Bhaktivedanta Swami Prabhupāda, 1896–1977. II. Title.
BL1124.7.I762E5 1993
294.5'9218—dc20 93-15792
CIP

CONTENTS

INTRODUCTION

"Teachings of the *Vedas*"

(*Delivered as a lecture by His Divine Grace A. C. Bhaktivedanta Swami Prabhupāda on October 6, 1969, at Conway Hall, London, England.*)

Ladies and gentlemen, today's subject matter is the teachings of the *Vedas*. What are the *Vedas*? The Sanskrit verbal root of *veda* can be interpreted variously, but the purport is finally one. *Veda* means knowledge. Any knowledge you accept is *veda,* for the teachings of the *Vedas* are the original knowledge. In the conditioned state, our knowledge is subjected to many deficiencies. The difference between a conditioned soul and a liberated soul is that the conditioned soul has four kinds of defects. The first defect is that he must commit mistakes. For example, in our country, Mahatma Gandhi was considered to be a very great personality, but he committed many mistakes. Even at the last stage of his life, his assistant warned, "Mahatma Gandhi, don't go to the New Delhi meeting. I have some friends, and I have heard there is danger." But he did not hear. He persisted in going and was killed. Even great personalities like Mahatma Gandhi, President Kennedy—there are so many of them—make mistakes. To err is human. This is one defect of the conditioned soul.

Another defect: to be illusioned. Illusion means to accept something which is not: *māyā*. *Māyā* means "what is not." Everyone is accepting the body as the self. If I ask you what you are, you will say, "I am Mr. John; I am a rich man; I am this; I am that." All these are bodily identifications. But you are not this body. This is illusion.

The third defect is the cheating propensity. Everyone has the propensity to cheat others. Although a person is fool number one, he poses himself as very intelligent. Although it is already pointed out that he is in illusion and makes mistakes, he will theorize: "I think this is this, this is this." But he does not even know his own position. He writes books of philosophy, although he is defective. That is his disease. That is cheating.

Lastly, our senses are imperfect. We are very proud of our eyes. Often, someone will challenge, "Can you show me God?" But do you have the eyes to see God? You will never see if you haven't the eyes. If immediately the room becomes dark, you cannot even see your hands. So what power do you have to see? We cannot, therefore, expect knowledge (*veda*) with these imperfect senses. With all these deficiencies, in conditioned life we cannot give perfect knowledge to anyone. Nor are we ourselves perfect. Therefore we accept the *Vedas* as they are.

You may call the *Vedas* Hindu, but "Hindu" is a foreign name. We are not Hindus. Our real identification is *varṇāśrama. Varṇāśrama* denotes the followers of the *Vedas,* those who accept the human society in eight divisions of *varṇa* and *āśrama*. There are four divisions of society and four divisions of spiritual life. This is called *varṇāśrama*. It is stated in the *Bhagavad-gītā,* "These divisions are everywhere because they are created by God." The divisions of society are *brāhmaṇa, kṣatriya, vaiśya, śūdra. Brāhmaṇa* refers to the very intelligent class of men, those who know what is Brahman. Similarly, the *kṣatriyas,* the administrator group, are the next intelligent class of men. Then the *vaiśyas,* the mercantile group. These natural classifications are found everywhere. This is the Vedic principle, and we accept it. Vedic principles are accepted as axiomatic truth, for there cannot be any mistake. That is acceptance. For instance, in India cow dung is accepted as pure, and yet cow dung is the stool of an animal. In one place you'll find the Vedic injunction that if you touch stool, you have to take a bath immediately. But in another place it is said that the stool of a cow is pure. If you smear cow dung in an impure place, that place becomes pure. With our ordinary sense we can argue, "This is contradictory." Actually, it is contradictory from the ordinary point of view, but it is not false. It is fact. In Calcutta, a very prominent scientist and doctor analyzed cow dung and found that it contains all antiseptic properties.

In India if one person tells another, "You must do this," the other party may say, "What do you mean? Is this a Vedic injunction, that I have to follow you without any argument?" Vedic injunctions cannot be interpreted. But ultimately, if you carefully study why these injunctions are there, you will find that they are all correct.

The *Vedas* are not compilations of human knowledge. Vedic knowledge comes from the spiritual world, from Lord Kṛṣṇa. Another name for the *Vedas* is *śruti*. *Śruti* refers to that knowledge which is acquired by hearing. It is not experimental knowledge. *Śruti* is considered to be like a mother. We take so much knowledge from our mother. For example, if you want to know who your father is, who can answer you? Your mother. If the mother says, "Here is your father," you have to accept it. It is not possible to experiment to find out whether he is your father. Similarly, if you want to know something beyond your experience, beyond your experimental knowledge, beyond the activities of the senses, then you have to accept the *Vedas*. There is no question of experimenting. It has already been experimented. It is already settled. The version of the mother, for instance, has to be accepted as truth. There is no other way.

The *Vedas* are considered to be the mother, and Brahmā is called the grandfather, the forefather, because he was the first to be instructed in the Vedic knowledge. In the beginning the first living creature was Brahmā. He received this Vedic knowledge and imparted it to Nārada and other disciples and sons, and they also distributed it to their disciples. In this way, the Vedic knowledge comes down by disciplic succession. It is also confirmed in the *Bhagavad-gītā* that Vedic knowledge is understood in this way. If you make experimental endeavor, you come to the same conclusion, but just to save time you should accept. If you want to know who your father is and if you accept your mother as the authority, then whatever she says can be accepted without argument. There are three kinds of evidence: *pratyakṣa, anumāna* and *śabda. Pratyakṣa* means "direct evidence." Direct evidence is not very good because our senses are not perfect. We are seeing the sun daily, and it appears to us just like a small disc, but it is actually far, far larger than many planets. Of what value is this seeing? Therefore we have to read books; then we can understand about the sun. So direct experience is not perfect. Then there is *anumāna,* inductive knowledge: "It may be like this"—hypothesis. For instance, Darwin's theory says it may be like this, it may be like that. But that is not science. That is a suggestion, and it is also not perfect. But if you receive the knowledge from the authoritative sources, that is perfect. If you receive a program guide from the radio station authorities, you accept it. You don't deny it; you don't have to make an experiment, because it is received from the authoritative sources.

Vedic knowledge is called *śabda-pramāṇa.* Another name is *śruti. Śruti* means that this knowledge has to be received simply by aural reception. The *Vedas* instruct that in order to understand transcendental knowledge, we have to hear from the authority. Transcendental knowledge is knowledge from beyond this universe. Within this universe is material knowledge, and beyond this universe is transcendental knowledge. We cannot even go to the end of the universe, so how can we go to the spiritual world? Thus to acquire full knowledge is impossible.

There is a spiritual sky. There is another nature, which is beyond manifestation and nonmanifestation. But how will you know that there is a sky where the planets and inhabitants are eternal? All this knowledge is there, but how will you make experiments? It is not possible. Therefore you have to take the assistance of the *Vedas*. This is called Vedic knowledge. In our Kṛṣṇa consciousness movement we are accepting knowledge from the highest authority, Kṛṣṇa. Kṛṣṇa is accepted as the highest authority by all classes of men. I am speaking first of the two classes of transcendentalists. One class of transcendentalists is called impersonalistic, Māyāvādī. They are generally known as Vedāntists, led by Śaṅkarācārya. And there is another class of transcendentalists, called Vaiṣṇavas, like Rāmānujācārya, Madhvācārya, Viṣṇu Svāmī. Both the Śaṅkara-sampradāya and the Vaiṣṇava *sampradāya* have accepted Kṛṣṇa as the Supreme Personality of Godhead. Śaṅkarācārya is supposed to be an impersonalist who preached impersonalism, impersonal Brahman, but it is a fact that he is a covered personalist. In his commentary on the *Bhagavad-gītā* he wrote, "Nārāyaṇa, the Supreme Personality of Godhead, is beyond this cosmic manifestation." And then again he confirmed, "That Supreme Personality of Godhead, Nārāyaṇa, is Kṛṣṇa. He has come as the son of Devakī and Vasudeva." He particularly mentioned the names of His father and mother. So Kṛṣṇa is accepted as the Supreme Personality of Godhead by all transcendentalists. There is no doubt about it. Our source of knowledge in Kṛṣṇa consciousness is the *Bhagavad-gītā*, which comes directly from Kṛṣṇa.

We have published *Bhagavad-gītā As It Is* because we accept Kṛṣṇa as He is speaking, without any interpretation. That is Vedic knowledge. Since the Vedic knowledge is pure, we accept it. Whatever Kṛṣṇa says, we accept. This is Kṛṣṇa consciousness. That saves much time. If you accept the right authority, or source of knowledge, then you save much time. For example, there are two systems of knowledge in the material world: inductive and deductive. From deductive, you accept that man is mortal. Your father says man is mortal, your sister says man is mortal, everyone says man is mortal—but you do not experiment. You accept it as a fact that man is mortal. If you want to research to find out whether man is mortal, you have to study each and every man, and you may come to think that there may be some man who is not dying but you have not seen him yet. So in this way your research will never be finished. In Sanskrit this process is called *āroha,* the ascending process. If you want to attain knowledge by any personal endeavor, by exercising your imperfect senses, you will never come to the right conclusions. That is not possible.

There is a statement in the *Brahma-saṁhitā:* Just ride on the airplane which runs at the speed of mind. Our material airplanes can run two thousand miles per hour, but what is the speed of mind? You are sitting at home, you immediately think of India—say, ten thousand miles away—and at once it is in your home. Your mind has gone there. The mind-speed is so swift. Therefore it is stated, "If you travel at this speed for millions of years, you'll find that the spiritual sky is unlimited." It is not possible even to approach it. Therefore, the Vedic injunction is that one must approach—the word "compulsory" is used—a bona fide spiritual master, a *guru.* And what is the qualification of a spiritual master? He is one who has rightly heard the Vedic message from the right source, and he must practically be firmly established in Brahman. These are the two qualities he must have. Otherwise he is not bona fide.

This Kṛṣṇa consciousness movement is completely authorized from Vedic principles. In the *Bhagavad-gītā* Kṛṣṇa says, "The actual aim of Vedic research is to find out Kṛṣṇa." In the *Brahma-saṁhitā* it is also stated, "Kṛṣṇa, Govinda, has innumerable forms, but they are all one." They are not like our forms, which are fallible. His form is infallible. My form has a beginning, but His form has no beginning. It is *ananta.* And His form—so many multiforms—has no end. My form is sitting here and not in my apartment. You are sitting there and not in your apartment. But Kṛṣṇa can be everywhere at one time. He can sit down in Goloka Vṛndāvana, and at the same time He is everywhere, all-pervading. He is original, the oldest, but whenever you look at a picture of Kṛṣṇa you'll find a young boy fifteen or twenty years old. You will never find an old man. You have seen pictures of Kṛṣṇa as a charioteer from the *Bhagavad-gītā.* At that time He was not less than one hundred years old. He had great-grandchildren, but He looked just like a boy. Kṛṣṇa, God, never becomes old. That is His supreme power. And if you want to search out Kṛṣṇa by studying the Vedic literature, then you will be baffled. It may be possible, but it is very difficult. But you can very easily learn about Him from His devotee. His devotee can deliver Him to you: "Here He is, take Him." That is the potency of Kṛṣṇa's devotees.

Originally there was only one *Veda,* and there was no necessity of reading it. People were so intelligent and had such sharp memories that by once hearing from the lips of the spiritual master they would understand. They would immediately grasp the whole purport. But five thousand years ago Vyāsadeva put the *Vedas* in writing for the people in this age, Kali-yuga. He knew that eventually the people would be short-lived, their memories would be very poor, and their intelligence would not be very sharp. "Therefore, let me teach this Vedic knowledge in writing." He divided the *Vedas* into four: *Ṛg, Sāma, Atharva* and *Yajur.* Then he gave the charge of these *Vedas* to his different disciples. He then thought of the less intelligent class of men-*strī, śūdra* and *dvija-bandhu.* He considered the woman class and *śūdra* class (worker class) and *dvija-bandhu. Dvija-bandhu* refers to those who are born in a high family but who are not properly qualified. A man who is born in the family of a *brāhmaṇa* but is not qualified as a *brāhmaṇa* is called *dvija-bandhu.* For these persons he compiled the *Mahābhārata,* called the history of India, and the eighteen *Purāṇas.* These are all part of the Vedic literature: the *Purāṇas,* the *Mahābhārata,* the four *Vedas* and the *Upaniṣads.* The *Upaniṣads* are part of the *Vedas.* Then Vyāsadeva summarized all Vedic knowledge for scholars and philosophers in what is called the *Vedānta-sūtra.* This is the last word of the *Vedas.*

Vyāsadeva personally wrote the *Vedānta-sūtra* under the instructions of Nārada, his Guru Mahārāja (spiritual master), but still he was not satisfied. That is a long story, described in *Śrīmad-Bhāgavatam.* Vedavyāsa was not very satisfied even after compiling many *Purāṇas* and *Upaniṣads,* and even after writing the *Vedānta-sūtra.* Then his spiritual master, Nārada, instructed him, "You explain the *Vedānta-sūtra.*" *Vedānta* means "ultimate knowledge," and the ultimate knowledge is Kṛṣṇa. Kṛṣṇa says that throughout all the *Vedas* one has to understand Him: *vedaiś ca sarvair aham eva vedyaḥ.* Kṛṣṇa also says, *vedānta-kṛd veda-vid eva cāham:* "I am the compiler of the *Vedānta-sūtra,* and I am the knower of the *Vedas.*" Therefore the ultimate objective is Kṛṣṇa. That is explained in all the Vaiṣṇava commentaries on Vedānta philosophy. We Gauḍīya Vaiṣṇavas have our commentary on Vedānta philosophy, called *Govinda-bhāṣya,* by Baladeva Vidyābhūṣaṇa. Similarly, Rāmānujācārya has a commentary, and Madhvācārya has one. The version of Śaṅkarācārya is not the only commentary. There are many *Vedānta* commentaries, but because the Vaiṣṇavas did not present the first *Vedānta* commentary, people are under the wrong impression that Śaṅkarācārya's is the only *Vedānta* commentary. Besides that, Vyāsadeva himself wrote the perfect *Vedānta* commentary, *Śrīmad-Bhāgavatam.* *Śrīmad-Bhāgavatam* begins with the first words of the *Vedānta-sūtra: janmādy asya yataḥ.* And that *janmādy asya yataḥ* is fully explained in *Śrīmad-Bhāgavatam.* The *Vedānta-sūtra* simply hints at what is Brahman, the Absolute Truth: "The Absolute Truth is that from whom everything emanates." This is a summary, but it is explained in detail in

Śrīmad-Bhāgavatam. If everything is emanating from the Absolute Truth, then what is the nature of the Absolute Truth? That is explained in *Śrīmad-Bhāgavatam.* The Absolute Truth must be consciousness. He is self-effulgent (*sva-rāṭ*). We develop our consciousness and knowledge by receiving knowledge from others, but for Him it is said that He is self-effulgent. The whole summary of Vedic knowledge is the *Vedānta-sūtra,* and the *Vedānta-sūtra* is explained by the writer himself in *Śrīmad-Bhāgavatam.* We finally request those who are actually after Vedic knowledge to try to understand the explanation of all Vedic knowledge from *Śrīmad-Bhāgavatam* and the *Bhagavad-gītā.*

INVOCATION

ॐ पूर्णमदः पूर्णमिदं पूर्णात् पूर्णमुदच्यते ।
पूर्णस्य पूर्णमादाय पूर्णमेवावशिष्यते ॥

oṁ pūrṇam adaḥ pūrṇam idaṁ
pūrṇāt pūrṇam udacyate
pūrṇasya pūrṇam ādāya
pūrṇam evāvaśiṣyate

oṁ—the Complete Whole; *pūrṇam*—perfectly complete; *adaḥ*—that; *pūrṇam*—perfectly complete; *idam*—this phenomenal world; *pūrṇāt*—from the all-perfect; *pūrṇam*—complete unit; *udacyate*—is produced; *pūrṇasya*—of the Complete Whole; *pūrṇam*—completely, all; *ādāya*—having been taken away; *pūrṇam*—the complete balance; *eva*—even; *avaśiṣyate*—is remaining.

TRANSLATION

The Personality of Godhead is perfect and complete, and because He is completely perfect, all emanations from Him, such as this phenomenal world, are perfectly equipped as complete wholes. Whatever is produced of the Complete Whole is also complete in itself. Because He is the Complete Whole, even though so many complete units emanate from Him, He remains the complete balance.

PURPORT

The Complete Whole, or the Supreme Absolute Truth, is the complete Personality of Godhead. Realization of impersonal Brahman or of Paramātmā, the Supersoul, is incomplete realization of the Absolute Complete. The Supreme Personality of Godhead is *sac-cid-ānanda-vigraha.* Realization of impersonal Brahman is realization of His *sat* feature, or His aspect of eternity, and Paramātmā realization is realization of His *sat* and *cit* features, His aspects of eternity and knowledge. But realization of the Personality of Godhead is realization of all the transcendental features—*sat, cit* and *ānanda,* bliss. When one realizes the Supreme Person, he realizes these aspects of the Absolute Truth in their completeness. *Vigraha* means "form." Thus the Complete Whole is not formless. If He were formless, or if He were less than His creation in any other way, He could not be complete. The Complete Whole must contain everything both within and beyond our experience; otherwise He cannot be complete.

The Complete Whole, the Personality of Godhead, has immense potencies, all of which are as complete as He is. Thus this phenomenal world is also complete in itself. The twenty-four elements of which this material universe is a temporary manifestation are arranged to produce everything necessary for the maintenance and subsistence of this universe. No other unit in the universe need make an extraneous effort to try to maintain the universe. The universe functions on its own time scale, which is fixed by the energy of the Complete Whole, and when that schedule is completed, this temporary manifestation will be annihilated by the complete arrangement of the Complete Whole.

All facilities are given to the small complete units (namely the living beings) to enable them to realize the Complete Whole. All forms of incompleteness are experienced due to incomplete knowledge of the Complete Whole. The human form of life is a complete manifestation of the consciousness of the living being, and it is obtained after evolving through 8,400,000 species of life in the cycle of birth and death. If in this human life of full consciousness the living entity does not realize his completeness in relation to the Complete Whole, he loses the chance to realize his completeness and is again put into the evolutionary cycle by the law of material nature.

Because we do not know that there is a complete arrangement in nature for our maintenance, we make efforts to utilize the resources of nature to create a so-called complete life of sense enjoyment. Because the living entity cannot enjoy the life of the senses without being dovetailed with the Complete Whole, the misleading life of sense enjoyment is illusion. The hand of a body is a complete unit only as long as it is attached to the complete body. When the hand is severed from the body, it may appear like a hand, but it actually has none of the potencies of a hand. Similarly, living beings are part and parcel of the Complete Whole, and if they are severed from the Complete Whole, the illusory representation of completeness cannot fully satisfy them.

The completeness of human life can be realized only when one engages in the service of the Complete Whole. All services in this world—whether social, political, communal, international or even interplanetary—will remain incomplete until they are dovetailed with the Complete Whole. When everything is dovetailed with the Complete Whole, the attached parts and parcels also become complete in themselves.

MANTRA ONE

ईशावास्यमिदꣳ सर्वं यत्किञ्च जगत्यां जगत्।
तेन त्यक्तेन भुञ्जीथा मा गृधः कस्य स्विद् धनम् ॥१॥

īśāvāsyam idaṁ sarvaṁ
yat kiñca jagatyāṁ jagat
tena tyaktena bhuñjīthā
mā gṛdhaḥ kasya svid dhanam

īśa—by the Lord; *āvāsyam*—controlled; *idam*—this; *sarvam*—all; *yat kiñca*—whatever; *jagatyām*—within the universe; *jagat*—all that is animate or inanimate; *tena*—by Him; *tyaktena*—set-apart quota; *bhuñjīthāḥ*—you should accept; *mā*—do not; *gṛdhaḥ*—endeavor to gain; *kasya svit*—of anyone else; *dhanam*—the wealth.

TRANSLATION

Everything animate or inanimate that is within the universe is controlled and owned by the Lord. One should therefore accept only those things necessary for himself, which are set aside as his quota, and one should not accept other things, knowing well to whom they belong.

PURPORT

Vedic knowledge is infallible because it comes down

through the perfect disciplic succession of spiritual masters, beginning with the Lord Himself. Since He spoke the first word of Vedic knowledge, the source of this knowledge is transcendental. The words spoken by the Lord are called *apauruṣeya,* which indicates that they are not delivered by any mundane person. A living being who lives in the mundane world has four defects: (1) he is certain to commit mistakes; (2) he is subject to illusion; (3) he has a propensity to cheat others; and (4) his senses are imperfect. No one with these four imperfections can deliver perfect knowledge. The *Vedas* are not produced by such an imperfect creature. Vedic knowledge was originally imparted by the Lord into the heart of Brahmā, the first created living being, and Brahmā in his turn disseminated this knowledge to his sons and disciples, who have handed it down through history.

Since the Lord is *pūrṇam,* all-perfect, there is no possibility of His being subjected to the laws of material nature, which He controls. However, both the living entities and inanimate objects are controlled by the laws of nature and ultimately by the Lord's potency. This *Īśopaniṣad* is part of the *Yajur Veda,* and consequently it contains information concerning the proprietorship of all things existing within the universe.

The Lord's proprietorship over everything within the universe is confirmed in the Seventh Chapter of the *Bhagavad-gītā* (7.4–5), where *parā* and *aparā prakṛti* are discussed. The elements of nature—earth, water, fire, air, ether, mind, intelligence and ego—all belong to the Lord's inferior, material energy (*aparā prakṛti*), whereas the living being, the organic energy, is His superior energy (*parā prakṛti*). Both of these *prakṛtis,* or energies, are emanations from the Lord, and ultimately He is the controller of everything that exists. There is nothing in the universe that does not belong to either the *parā* or the *aparā prakṛti;* therefore everything is the property of the Supreme Being.

Because the Supreme Being, the Absolute Personality of Godhead, is the complete person, He has complete and perfect intelligence to adjust everything by means of His different potencies. The Supreme Being is often compared to a fire, and everything organic and inorganic is compared to the heat and light of that fire. Just as fire distributes energy in the form of heat and light, the Lord displays His energy in different ways. He thus remains the ultimate controller, sustainer and dictator of everything. He is the possessor of all potencies, the knower of everything and the benefactor of everyone. He is full of inconceivable opulence, power, fame, beauty, knowledge and renunciation.

One should therefore be intelligent enough to know that except for the Lord no one is a proprietor of anything. One should accept only those things that are set aside by the Lord as his quota. The cow, for instance, gives milk, but she does not drink that milk: she eats grass and straw, and her milk is designated as food for human beings. Such is the arrangement of the Lord. Thus we should be satisfied with those things He has kindly set aside for us, and we should always consider to whom those things we possess actually belong.

Take, for example, our dwelling, which is made of

earth, wood, stone, iron, cement and so many other material things. If we think in terms of *Śrī Īśopaniṣad,* we must know that we cannot produce any of these building materials ourselves. We can simply bring them together and transform them into different shapes by our labor. A laborer cannot claim to be a proprietor of a thing just because he has worked hard to manufacture it.

In modern society there is always a great quarrel between the laborers and the capitalists. This quarrel has taken an international shape, and the world is in danger. Men face one another in enmity and snarl just like cats and dogs. *Śrī Īśopaniṣad* cannot give advice to the cats and dogs, but it can deliver the message of Godhead to man through the bona fide *ācāryas* (holy teachers). The human race should take the Vedic wisdom of *Śrī Īśopaniṣad* and not quarrel over material possessions. One must be satisfied with whatever privileges are given to him by the mercy of the Lord. There can be no peace if the communists or capitalists or any other party claims proprietorship over the resources of nature, which are entirely the property of the Lord. The capitalists cannot curb the communists simply by political maneuvering, nor can the communists defeat the capitalists simply by fighting for stolen bread. If they do not recognize the proprietorship of the Supreme Personality of Godhead, all the property they claim to be their own is stolen. Consequently they will be liable to punishment by the laws of nature. Nuclear bombs are in the hands of both communists and capitalists, and if both do not recognize the proprietorship of the Supreme Lord, it is certain that these bombs will ultimately ruin both parties. Thus in order to save themselves and bring peace to the world, both parties must follow the instructions of *Śrī Īśopaniṣad*.

Human beings are not meant to quarrel like cats and dogs. They must be intelligent enough to realize the importance and aim of human life. The Vedic literature is meant for humanity and not for cats and dogs. Cats and dogs can kill other animals for food without incurring sin, but if a man kills an animal for the satisfaction of his uncontrolled taste buds, he is responsible for breaking the laws of nature. Consequently he must be punished.

The standard of life for human beings cannot be applied to animals. The tiger does not eat rice and wheat or drink cow's milk, because he has been given food in the shape of animal flesh. Among the many animals and birds, some are vegetarian and others are carnivorous, but none of them transgress the laws of nature, which have been ordained by the will of the Lord. Animals, birds, reptiles and other lower life forms strictly adhere to the laws of nature; therefore there is no question of sin for them, nor are the Vedic instructions meant for them. Human life alone is a life of responsibility.

It is wrong, however, to think that simply by becoming a vegetarian one can avoid transgressing the laws of nature. Vegetables also have life, and while it is nature's law that one living being is meant to feed on another, for human beings the point is to recognize the Supreme Lord. Thus one should not be proud of being a strict vegetarian. Animals do not have developed consciousness by which to recognize the Lord, but a human being is sufficiently intelligent to take lessons from the Vedic literature and thereby know how the laws of nature are working and derive profit out of such knowledge. If a man neglects the instructions of the Vedic literature, his life becomes very risky. A human being is therefore required to recognize the authority of the Supreme Lord and become His devotee. He must offer everything for the Lord's service and partake only of the remnants of food offered to the Lord. This will enable him to discharge his duty properly. In the *Bhagavad-gītā* (9.26) the Lord directly states that He accepts vegetarian food from the hands of a pure devotee. Therefore a human being should not only become a strict vegetarian but should also become a devotee of the Lord, offer the Lord all his food and then partake of such *prasādam,* or the mercy of God. Only those who act in this way can properly discharge the duties of human life. Those who do not offer their food to the Lord eat nothing but sin and subject themselves to various types of distress, which are the results of sin (Bg. 3.13).

The root of sin is deliberate disobedience to the laws of nature through disregarding the proprietorship of the Lord. Disobeying the laws of nature or the order of the Lord brings ruin to a human being. Conversely, one who is sober, who knows the laws of nature, and who is not influenced by unnecessary attachment or aversion is sure to be recognized by the Lord and thus become eligible to go back to Godhead, back to the eternal home.

MANTRA TWO

कुर्वन्नेवेह कर्माणि जिजीविषेच्छतꣳ समाः ।
एवं त्वयि नान्यथेतोऽस्ति न कर्म लिप्यते नरे ॥२॥

kurvann eveha karmāṇi
jijīviṣec chataṁ samāḥ
evaṁ tvayi nānyatheto 'sti
na karma lipyate nare

kurvan—doing continuously; *eva*—thus; *iha*—during this span of life; *karmāṇi*—work; *jijīviṣet*—one should desire to live; *śatam*—one hundred; *samāḥ*—years; *evam*—so living; *tvayi*—unto you; *na*—no; *anyathā*—alternative; *itaḥ*—from this path; *asti*—there is; *na*—not; *karma*—work; *lipyate*—can be bound; *nare*—unto a man.

TRANSLATION

One may aspire to live for hundreds of years if he continuously goes on working in that way, for that sort of work will not bind him to the law of karma. There is no alternative to this way for man.

PURPORT

No one wants to die: everyone wants to live as long as he can drag on. This tendency is visible not only individually but also collectively in the community, society and nation. There is a hard struggle for life by all kinds of living entities, and the *Vedas* say that this is quite natural. The living being is eternal by nature, but due to his bondage in material existence he has to change his body over and over. This process is called transmigration of the soul or *karma-bandhana,* bondage by one's work. The living entity has to work for his livelihood because that is the law of material nature, and if he does not act according to his prescribed duties, he transgresses the law of nature and binds himself more and more to the cycle of birth and death in the many species of life.

Other life forms are also subject to the cycle of birth and death, but when the living entity attains a human life, he gets a chance to get free from the chains of *karma. Karma, akarma* and *vikarma* are very clearly described in the *Bhagavad-gītā.* Actions that are performed in terms of one's prescribed duties, as mentioned in the revealed scriptures, are called *karma.* Actions that free one from the cycle of birth and death are called *akarma.* And actions that are performed through the misuse of one's freedom and that direct one to the lower life forms are called *vikarma.* Of these three types of action, that which frees one from the bondage to *karma* is preferred by intelligent men. Ordinary men wish to perform good work in order to be recognized and achieve some higher status of life in this world or in heaven, but more advanced men want to be free altogether from the actions and reactions of work. Intelligent men well know that both good and bad work equally bind one to the material miseries. Consequently they seek that work which will free them from the reactions of both good and bad work. Such liberating work is described here in the pages of *Śrī Īśopaniṣad.*

The instructions of *Śrī Īśopaniṣad* are more elaborately explained in the *Bhagavad-gītā,* sometimes called the *Gītopaniṣad,* the cream of all the *Upaniṣads.* In the *Bhagavad-gītā* (3.9–16) the Personality of Godhead says that one cannot attain the state of *naiṣkarmya,* or *akarma,* without executing the prescribed duties mentioned in the Vedic literature. This literature can regulate the working energy of a human being in such a way that he can gradually realize the authority of the Supreme Being. When he realizes the authority of the Personality of Godhead—Vāsudeva, or Kṛṣṇa—it is to be understood that he has attained the stage of positive knowledge. In this purified stage the modes of nature—namely goodness, passion and ignorance—cannot act, and he is able to work on the basis of *naiṣkarmya.* Such work does not bind one to the cycle of birth and death.

Factually, no one has to do anything more than render devotional service to the Lord. However, in the lower stages of life one cannot immediately adopt the activities of devotional service, nor can one completely stop fruitive work. A conditioned soul is accustomed to working for sense gratification—for his own selfish interest, immediate or extended. An ordinary man works for his own sense enjoyment, and when this principle of sense enjoyment is extended to include his society, nation or humanity in general, it assumes various attractive names such as altruism, socialism, communism, nationalism and humanitarianism. These "isms" are certainly very attractive forms of *karma-bandhana* (karmic bondage), but the Vedic instruction of *Śrī Īśopaniṣad* is that if one actually wants to live for any of the above "isms," he should make them God-centered. There is no harm in becoming a family man, or an altruist, a socialist, a communist, a nationalist or a humanitarian, provided that one executes his activities in relation with *īśāvāsya,* the God-centered conception.

In the *Bhagavad-gītā* (2.40) Lord Kṛṣṇa states that God-centered activities are so valuable that just a few of them can save a person from the greatest danger. The greatest danger of life is the danger of gliding down again into the evolutionary cycle of birth and death among the 8,400,000 species. If somehow or other a man misses the spiritual opportunity afforded by his human form of life and falls down again into the evolutionary cycle, he must be considered most unfortunate. Due to his defective senses, a foolish man cannot see that this is happening. Consequently *Śrī Īśopaniṣad* advises us to exert our energy in the spirit of *īśāvāsya.* Being so engaged, we may wish to live for many, many years; otherwise a long life in itself has no value. A tree lives for hundreds and hundreds of years, but there is no point in living a long time like trees, or breathing like bellows, or begetting children like hogs and dogs, or eating like camels. A humble God-centered life is more valuable than a colossal hoax of a life dedicated to godless altruism or socialism.

When altruistic activities are executed in the spirit of *Śrī Īśopaniṣad,* they become a form of *karma-yoga.* Such activities are recommended in the *Bhagavad-gītā* (18.5–9), for they guarantee their executor protection from the danger of sliding down into the evolutionary process of birth and death. Even though such God-centered activities may be half-finished, they are still good for the executor because they will guarantee him a human form in his next birth. In this way one can have another chance to improve his position on the path of liberation.

How one can execute God-centered activities is elaborately explained in the *Bhakti-rasāmṛta-sindhu,* by Śrīla Rūpa Gosvāmī. We have rendered this book into English as *The Nectar of Devotion.* We recommend this valuable book to all who are interested in performing their activities in the spirit of *Śrī Īśopaniṣad.*

MANTRA THREE

असुर्या नाम ते लोका अन्धेन तमसावृताः ।
ताꣳस्ते प्रेत्याभिगच्छन्ति ये के चात्महनो जनाः ॥३॥

asuryā nāma te lokā
andhena tamasāvṛtāḥ
tām̐s te pretyābhigacchanti
ye ke cātma-hano janāḥ

asuryāḥ—meant for the *asuras; nāma*—famous by the name; *te*—those; *lokāḥ*—planets; *andhena*—by ignorance; *tamasā*—by darkness; *āvṛtāḥ*—covered; *tān*—those planets; *te*—they; *pretya*—after death; *abhigacchanti*—enter into; *ye*—anyone; *ke*—everyone; *ca*—and; *ātma-hanaḥ*—the killers of the soul; *janāḥ*—persons.

TRANSLATION

The killer of the soul, whoever he may be, must enter into the planets known as the worlds of the faithless, full of darkness and ignorance.

PURPORT

Human life is distinguished from animal life due to its heavy responsibilities. Those who are cognizant of these responsibilities and who work in that spirit are called *suras* (godly persons), and those who are neglectful of these responsibilities or who have no information of them are called *asuras* (demons). Throughout the universe there are only these two types of human beings. In the *Ṛg Veda* it is stated that the *suras* always aim at the lotus feet of the Supreme Lord Viṣṇu and act accordingly. Their ways are as illuminated as the path of the sun.

Intelligent human beings must always remember that the soul obtains a human form after an evolution of many millions of years in the cycle of transmigration. The material world is sometimes compared to an ocean, and the human body is compared to a solid boat designed especially to cross this ocean. The Vedic scriptures and the *ācāryas,* or saintly teachers, are compared to expert boatmen, and the facilities of the human body are compared to favorable breezes that help the boat ply smoothly to its desired destination. If, with all these facilities, a human being does not fully utilize his life for self-realization, he must be considered an *ātma-hā,* a killer of the soul. *Śrī Īśopaniṣad* warns in clear terms that the killer of the soul is destined to enter into the darkest region of ignorance to suffer perpetually.

There are swine, dogs, camels, asses, etc., whose economic necessities are just as important to them as ours are to us, but the economic problems of these animals are solved only under nasty and unpleasant conditions. The human being is given all facilities for a comfortable life by the laws of nature because the human form of life is more important and valuable than animal life. Why is man given a better life than that of the swine and other animals? Why is a highly placed government servant given better facilities than those of an ordinary clerk? The answer is that a highly placed officer has to discharge duties of a higher nature. Similarly, the duties human beings have to perform are higher than those of animals, who are always engaged in simply feeding their hungry stomachs. Yet the modern soul-killing civilization has only increased the problems of the hungry stomach. When we approach a polished animal in the form of a modern civilized man and ask him to take interest in self-realization, he will say that he simply wants to work to satisfy his stomach and that there is no need of self-realization for a hungry man. The laws of nature are so cruel, however, that despite his denunciation of the need for self-realization and his eagerness to work hard to fill his stomach, he is always threatened by unemployment.

We are given this human form of life not to work hard like asses, swine and dogs but to attain the highest perfection of life. If we do not care for self-realization, the laws of nature force us to work very hard, even though we may not want to do so. Human beings in this age have been forced to work hard like the asses and bullocks that pull carts. Some of the regions where the *asuras* are sent to work are revealed in this *mantra* of *Śrī Īśopaniṣad*. If a man fails to discharge his duties as a human being, he is forced to transmigrate to the *asurya* planets and take birth in degraded species of life to work hard in ignorance and darkness.

In the *Bhagavad-gītā* (6.41–43) it is stated that a man who enters upon the path of self-realization but does not complete the process, despite having sincerely tried to realize his relationship with God, is given a chance to appear in a family of *śuci* or *śrīmat.* The word *śuci* indicates a spiritually advanced *brāhmaṇa,* and *śrīmat* indicates a *vaiśya,* a member of the mercantile community. So the person who fails to achieve self-realization is given a better chance in his next life due to his sincere efforts in this life. If even a fallen candidate is given a chance to take birth in a respectable and noble family, one can hardly imagine the status of one who has achieved success. By simply attempting to realize God, one is guaranteed birth in a wealthy or aristocratic family. But those who do not even make an attempt, who want to be covered by illusion, who are too materialistic and too attached to material enjoyment, must enter into the darkest regions of hell, as confirmed throughout the Vedic literature. Such materialistic *asuras* sometimes make a show of religion, but their ultimate aim is material prosperity. The *Bhagavad-gītā* (16.17–18) rebukes such men by calling them *ātma-sambhāvitā,* meaning that they are considered great only on the strength of deception and are empowered by the votes of the ignorant and by their own material wealth. Such *asuras,* devoid of self-realization and knowledge of *īśāvāsya,* the Lord's universal proprietorship, are certain to enter into the darkest regions.

The conclusion is that as human beings we are meant not simply for solving economic problems on a tottering platform but for solving all the problems of the material life into which we have been placed by the laws of nature.

MANTRA FOUR

अनेजदेकं मनसो जवीयो नैनद्देवा आप्नुवन् पूर्वमर्षत् ।
तद्धावतोऽन्यानत्येति तिष्ठत्तस्मिन्नपो मातरिश्वा दधाति ॥४॥

anejad ekaṁ manaso javīyo
nainad devā āpnuvan pūrvam arṣat
tad dhāvato 'nyān atyeti tiṣṭhat
tasminn apo mātariśvā dadhāti

anejat—fixed; *ekam*—one; *manasaḥ*—than the mind; *javīyaḥ*—more swift; *na*—not; *enat*—this Supreme Lord; *devāḥ*—the demigods like Indra, etc.; *āpnuvan*—can approach; *pūrvam*—in front; *arṣat*—moving quickly; *tat*—He; *dhāvataḥ*—those who are running; *anyān*—others; *atyeti*—surpasses; *tiṣṭhat*—remaining in one place; *tasmin*—in Him; *apaḥ*—rain; *mātariśvā*—the gods who control the wind and rain; *dadhāti*—supply.

TRANSLATION

Although fixed in His abode, the Personality of Godhead is swifter than the mind and can overcome all others running. The powerful demigods cannot approach Him. Although in one place, He controls those who supply the air and rain. He surpasses all in excellence.

PURPORT

Through mental speculation, even the greatest philosopher cannot know the Supreme Lord, who is the Absolute Personality of Godhead. He can be known only by His devotees through His mercy. In the *Brahma-saṁhitā* (5.34) it is stated that even if a nondevotee philosopher travels through space at the speed of the wind or the mind for hundreds of millions of years, he will still find that the Absolute Truth is far, far away from him. The *Brahma-saṁhitā* (5.37) further describes that the Absolute Personality of Godhead has His transcendental abode, known as Goloka, where He remains and engages in His pastimes, yet by His inconceivable potencies He can simultaneously reach every part of His creative energy. In the *Viṣṇu Purāṇa* His potencies are compared to the heat and light that emanate from a fire. Although situated in one place, a fire can distribute its light and heat for some distance; similarly, the Absolute Personality of Godhead, although fixed in His transcendental abode, can diffuse His different energies everywhere.

Although His energies are innumerable, they can be divided into three principal categories: the internal potency, the marginal potency and the external potency. There are hundreds and millions of subheadings to each of these categories. The dominating demigods who are empowered to control and administer such natural phenomena as air, light and rain are all classified within the marginal potency of the Absolute Person. Lesser living beings, including humans, also belong to the Lord's marginal potency. The material world is the creation of the Lord's external potency. And the spiritual sky, where the kingdom of God is situated, is the manifestation of His internal potency.

Thus the different energies of the Lord are present everywhere. Although the Lord and His energies are nondifferent, one should not mistake these energies for the Supreme Truth. Nor should one wrongly consider that the Supreme Lord is distributed everywhere impersonally or that He loses His personal existence. Men are accustomed to reaching conclusions according to their capacity for understanding, but the Supreme Lord is not subject to our limited capacity for understanding. It is for this reason that the *Upaniṣads* warn us that no one can approach the Lord by his own limited potency.

In the *Bhagavad-gītā* (10.2) the Lord says that not even the great *ṛṣis* and *suras* can know Him. And what to speak of the *asuras,* for whom there is no question of understanding the ways of the Lord? This fourth *mantra* of *Śrī Īśopaniṣad* very clearly suggests that the Absolute Truth is ultimately the Absolute Person; otherwise there would have been no need to mention so many details in support of His personal features.

Although the individual parts and parcels of the Lord's marginal potency have all the symptoms of the Lord Himself, they have limited spheres of activity and are therefore all limited. The parts and parcels are never equal to the whole; therefore they cannot appreciate the Lord's full potency. Under the influence of material nature, foolish and ignorant living beings who are but parts and parcels of the Lord try to conjecture about the Lord's transcendental position. *Śrī Īśopaniṣad* warns of the futility of trying to establish the identity of the Lord through mental speculation. One should try to learn of the Transcendence from the Lord Himself, the supreme source of the *Vedas,* for the Lord alone has full knowledge of the Transcendence.

Every part and parcel of the Complete Whole is endowed with some particular energy to act according to the Lord's will. When the part-and-parcel living entity forgets his particular activities under the Lord's will, he is considered to be in *māyā,* illusion. Thus from the very beginning *Śrī Īśopaniṣad* warns us to be very careful to play the part designated for us by the Lord. This does not mean that the individual soul has no initiative of his own. Because he is part and parcel of the Lord, he must partake of the initiative of the Lord as well. When a person properly utilizes his initiative, or active nature, with intelligence, understanding that everything is the Lord's potency, he can revive his original consciousness, which was lost due to association with *māyā,* the external energy.

All power is obtained from the Lord; therefore each particular power must be utilized to execute the will of the Lord and not otherwise. The Lord can be known by one who has adopted such a submissive service attitude. Perfect knowledge means knowing the Lord in all His features, knowing His potencies and knowing how these potencies work by His will. These matters are described by the Lord in the *Bhagavad-gītā,* the essence of all the *Upaniṣads.*

MANTRA FIVE

तदेजति तन्नैजति तद् दूरे तद्वन्तिके ।
तदन्तरस्य सर्वस्य तदु सर्वस्यास्य बाह्यतः ॥५॥

tad ejati tan naijati
tad dūre tad v antike
tad antar asya sarvasya
tad u sarvasyāsya bāhyataḥ

tat—this Supreme Lord; *ejati*—walks; *tat*—He; *na*—not; *ejati*—walks; *tat*—He; *dūre*—far away; *tat*—He; *u*—also; *antike*—very near; *tat*—He; *antaḥ*—within; *asya*—of this; *sarvasya*—of all; *tat*—He; *u*—also; *sarvasya*—of all; *asya*—of this; *bāhyataḥ*—external to.

TRANSLATION

The Supreme Lord walks and does not walk. He is far away, but He is very near as well. He is within everything, and yet He is outside of everything.

PURPORT

Here is a description of some of the Supreme Lord's transcendental activities, executed by His inconceivable potencies. The contradictions given here prove the inconceivable potencies of the Lord. "He walks, and He does not walk." Ordinarily, if someone can walk, it is illogical to say he cannot walk. But in reference to God, such a contradiction simply serves to indicate His inconceivable power. With our limited fund of knowledge we cannot accommodate such contradictions, and therefore we conceive of the Lord in terms of our limited powers of understanding. For example, the impersonalist philosophers of the Māyāvāda school accept only the Lord's impersonal activities and reject His personal feature. But the members of the *Bhāgavata* school, adopting the perfect conception of the Lord, accept His inconceivable potencies and thus understand that He is both personal and impersonal. The *bhāgavatas* know that without inconceivable potencies there can be no meaning to the words "Supreme Lord."

We should not take it for granted that because we cannot see God with our eyes the Lord has no personal existence. *Śrī Īśopaniṣad* refutes this argument by declaring that the Lord is far away but very near also. The abode of the Lord is beyond the material sky, and we have no means to measure even this material sky. If the material sky extends so far, then what to speak of the spiritual sky, which is altogether beyond it? That the spiritual sky is situated far, far away from the material universe is confirmed in the *Bhagavad-gītā* (15.6). But despite the Lord's being so far away, He can at once, within less than a second, descend before us with a speed swifter than that of the mind or wind. He can also run so swiftly that no one can surpass Him. This has already been described in the previous *mantra*.

Yet when the Personality of Godhead comes before us, we neglect Him. Such foolish negligence is condemned by the Lord in the *Bhagavad-gītā* (9.11), where He says that the foolish deride Him, considering Him a mortal being. He is not a mortal being, nor does He come before us with a body produced of material nature. There are many so-called scholars who contend that the Lord descends in a body made of matter, just like an ordinary living being. Not knowing His inconceivable power, such foolish men place the Lord on an equal level with ordinary men.

Because He is full of inconceivable potencies, God can accept our service through any sort of medium, and He can convert His different potencies according to His own will. Nonbelievers argue either that the Lord cannot incarnate Himself at all, or that if He does He descends in a form of material energy. These arguments are nullified if we accept the existence of the Lord's inconceivable potencies. Then we will understand that even if the Lord appears before us in the form of material energy, it is quite possible for Him to convert this energy into spiritual energy. Since the source of the energies is one and the same, the energies can be utilized according to the will of their source. For example, the Lord can appear in the form of the *arcā-vigraha,* a Deity supposedly made of earth, stone or wood. Deity forms, although engraved from wood, stone or other matter, are not idols, as the iconoclasts contend.

In our present state of imperfect material existence, we cannot see the Supreme Lord due to imperfect vision. Yet those devotees who want to see Him by means of material vision are favored by the Lord, who appears in a so-called material form to accept His devotees' service. One should not think that such devotees, who are in the lowest stage of devotional service, are worshiping an idol. They are factually worshiping the Lord, who has agreed to appear before them in an approachable way. Nor is the *arcā* form fashioned according to the whims of the worshiper. This form is eternally existent with all paraphernalia. This can be actually felt by a sincere devotee, but not by an atheist.

In the *Bhagavad-gītā* (4.11) the Lord says that how He treats His devotee depends on the devotee's degree of surrender. The Lord reserves the right not to reveal Himself to anyone and everyone but to show Himself only to those souls who surrender unto Him. Thus for the surrendered soul He is always within reach, whereas for the unsurrendered soul He is far, far away and cannot be approached.

In this connection, two words the revealed scriptures often apply to the Lord—*saguṇa* ("with qualities") and *nirguṇa* ("without qualities")—are very important. The word *saguṇa* does not imply that when the Lord appears with perceivable qualities He must take on a material form and be subject to the laws of material nature. For Him there is no difference between the material and spiritual energies, because He is the source of all energies. As the controller of all energies, He cannot at any time be under their influence, as we are. The material energy works according to His direction; therefore He can use that energy for His purposes without ever being influenced by any of the qualities of that energy. (In this sense He is *nirguṇa*, "without qualities.") Nor does the Lord become a formless entity at any time, for ultimately He is the eternal form, the primeval

Lord. His impersonal aspect, or Brahman effulgence, is but the glow of His personal rays, just as the sun's rays are the glow of the sun-god.

When the child saint Prahlāda Mahārāja was in the presence of his atheist father, his father asked him, "Where is your God?" When Prahlāda replied that God resides everywhere, the father angrily asked whether his God was within one of the pillars of the palace, and the child said yes. At once the atheist king shattered the pillar in front of him to pieces, and the Lord instantly appeared as Nṛsiṁha, the half-man, half-lion incarnation, and killed the atheist king. Thus the Lord is within everything, and He creates everything by His different energies. Through His inconceivable powers He can appear at any place in order to favor His sincere devotee. Lord Nṛsiṁha appeared from within the pillar not by the order of the atheist king but by the wish of His devotee Prahlāda. An atheist cannot order the Lord to appear, but the Lord will appear anywhere and everywhere to show mercy to His devotee. The *Bhagavad-gītā* (4.8) similarly states that the Lord appears in order to vanquish nonbelievers and protect believers. Of course, the Lord has sufficient energies and agents who can vanquish atheists, but it pleases Him to personally favor a devotee. Therefore He descends as an incarnation. Actually, He descends only to favor His devotees and not for any other purpose.

In the *Brahma-saṁhitā* (5.35) it is said that Govinda, the primeval Lord, enters everything by His plenary portion. He enters the universe as well as all the atoms of the universe. He is outside in His *virāṭ* form, and He is within everything as *antaryāmī.* As *antaryāmī* He witnesses everything that is going on, and He awards us the results of our actions as *karma-phala.* We ourselves may forget what we have done in previous lives, but because the Lord witnesses our actions, the results of our actions are always there, and we have to undergo the reactions nonetheless.

The fact is that there is nothing but God within and without. Everything is a manifestation of His different energies, like the heat and light emanating from a fire, and in this way there is a oneness among His diverse energies. Although there is oneness, however, the Lord in His personal form still enjoys unlimitedly all the pleasures enjoyed minutely by the tiny part-and-parcel living entities.

MANTRA SIX

यस्तु सर्वाणि भूतान्यात्मन्येवानुपश्यति ।
सर्वभूतेषु चात्मानं ततो न विजुगुप्सते ॥६॥

yas tu sarvāṇi bhūtāny
ātmany evānupaśyati
sarva-bhūteṣu cātmānaṁ
tato na vijugupsate

yaḥ—he who; *tu*—but; *sarvāṇi*—all; *bhūtāni*—living entities; *ātmani*—in relation to the Supreme Lord; *eva*—only; *anupaśyati*—observes in a systematic way; *sarva-bhūteṣu*—in every living being; *ca*—and; *ātmānam*—the Supersoul; *tataḥ*—thereafter; *na*—not; *vijugupsate*—hates anyone.

TRANSLATION

He who systematically sees everything in relation to the Supreme Lord, who sees all living entities as His parts and parcels, and who sees the Supreme Lord within everything never hates anything or any being.

PURPORT

This is a description of the *mahā-bhāgavata,* the great personality who sees everything in relation to the Supreme Personality of Godhead. The Supreme Lord's presence is realized in three stages. The *kaniṣṭha-adhikārī* is in the lowest stage of realization. He goes to a place of worship, such as a temple, church or mosque, according to his religious faith, and worships there according to scriptural injunctions. Devotees in this stage consider the Lord to be present at the place of worship and nowhere else. They cannot ascertain who is in what position in devotional service, nor can they tell who has realized the Supreme Lord. Such devotees follow the routine formulas and sometimes quarrel among themselves, considering one type of devotion better than another. These *kaniṣṭha-adhikārīs* are actually materialistic devotees who are simply trying to transcend the material boundary to reach the spiritual plane.

Those who have attained the second stage of realization are called *madhyama-adhikārīs*. These devotees observe the distinctions between four categories of beings: (1) the Supreme Lord; (2) the devotees of the Lord; (3) the innocent, who have no knowledge of the Lord; and (4) the atheists, who have no faith in the Lord and hate those in devotional service. The *madhyama-adhikārī* behaves differently toward these four classes of person. He adores the Lord, considering Him the object of love, he makes friends with those who are in devotional service, he tries to awaken the dormant love of God in the hearts of the innocent, and he avoids the atheists, who deride the very name of the Lord.

Above the *madhyama-adhikārī* is the *uttama-adhikārī*, who sees everything in relation to the Supreme Lord. Such a devotee does not discriminate between an atheist and a theist but sees everyone as part and parcel of God. He knows that there is no essential difference between a vastly learned *brāhmaṇa* and a dog in the street, because both of them are part and parcel of the Lord, although they are encaged in different bodies on account of the different qualities of their activities in their previous lives. He sees that the *brāhmaṇa* particle of the Supreme Lord has not misused his little independence given him by the Lord and that the dog particle has misused his independence and is therefore being punished by the laws of nature by being encaged in the form of a dog. Not considering the respective actions of the *brāhmaṇa* and the dog, the *uttama-adhikārī* tries to do good to both. Such a learned devotee is not misled by material bodies but is attracted by the spiritual spark within them.

Those who imitate an *uttama-adhikārī* by flaunting a sense of oneness or fellowship but who behave on the bodily platform are actually false philanthropists. The conception of universal brotherhood must be learned from an *uttama-adhikārī* and not from a foolish person who does not properly understand the individual soul or the Supreme Lord's Supersoul expansion, who dwells everywhere.

It is clearly mentioned in this sixth *mantra* that one should "observe," or systematically see. This means that one must follow the previous *ācāryas,* the perfected teachers. *Anupaśyati* is the exact Sanskrit word used in this connection. *Anu* means "to follow," and *paśyati* means "to observe." Thus the word *anupaśyati* means that one should not see things as he does with the naked eye but should follow the previous *ācāryas.* Due to material defects, the naked eye cannot see anything properly. One cannot see properly unless one has heard from a superior source, and the highest source is the Vedic wisdom, which is spoken by the Lord Himself. Vedic truths are coming in disciplic succession from the Lord to Brahmā, from Brahmā to Nārada, from Nārada to Vyāsa, and from Vyāsa to his many disciples. Formerly there was no need to record the messages of the *Vedas,* because people in earlier ages were more intelligent and had sharper memories. They could follow the instructions simply by hearing once from the mouth of a bona fide spiritual master.

At present there are many commentaries on the revealed scriptures, but most of them are not in the line of disciplic succession coming from Śrīla Vyāsadeva, who originally compiled the Vedic wisdom. The final, most perfect and sublime work by Śrīla Vyāsadeva is *Śrīmad-Bhāgavatam,* which is the natural commentary on the *Vedānta-sūtra.* There is also the *Bhagavad-gītā,* which was spoken by the Lord Himself and recorded by Vyāsadeva. These are the most important revealed scriptures, and any commentary that contradicts the principles of the *Bhagavad-gītā* or *Śrīmad-Bhāgavatam* is unauthorized. There is complete agreement among the *Upaniṣads, Vedānta-sūtra, Vedas, Bhagavad-gītā* and *Śrīmad-Bhāgavatam,* and no one should try to reach any conclusion about the *Vedas* without receiving instructions from members of Vyāsadeva's disciplic succession, who believe in the Personality of Godhead and His diverse energies as they are explained in *Śrī Īśopaniṣad.*

According to the *Bhagavad-gītā* (18.54), only one

who is already on the liberated platform (*brahma-bhūta*) can become an *uttama-adhikārī* devotee and see every living being as his own brother. This vision cannot be had by politicians, who are always after some material gain. One who imitates the symptoms of an *uttama-adhikārī* may serve another's outward body for the purpose of fame or material reward, but he does not serve the spirit soul. Such an imitator can have no information of the spiritual world. The *uttama-adhikārī* sees the spirit soul within the material body and serves him as spirit. Thus the material aspect is automatically served.

MANTRA SEVEN

यस्मिन् सर्वाणि भूतान्यात्मैवाभूद् विजानतः ।
तत्र को मोहः कः शोक एकत्वमनुपश्यतः ॥७॥

yasmin sarvāṇi bhūtāny
ātmaivābhūd vijānataḥ
tatra ko mohaḥ kaḥ śoka
ekatvam anupaśyataḥ

yasmin—in the situation; *sarvāṇi*—all; *bhūtāni*—living entities; *ātmā*—the *cit-kaṇa,* or spiritual spark; *eva*—only; *abhūt*—exist as; *vijānataḥ*—of one who knows; *tatra*—therein; *kaḥ*—what; *mohaḥ*—illusion; *kaḥ*—what; *śokaḥ*—anxiety; *ekatvam*—oneness in quality; *anupaśyataḥ*—of one who sees through authority, or one who sees constantly like that.

TRANSLATION

One who always sees all living entities as spiritual sparks, in quality one with the Lord, becomes a true knower of things. What, then, can be illusion or anxiety for him?

PURPORT

Except for the *madhyama-adhikārī* and *uttama-adhikārī* discussed above, no one can correctly see the spiritual position of a living being. The living entities are qualitatively one with the Supreme Lord, just as the sparks of a fire are qualitatively one with the fire. Yet sparks are not fire as far as quantity is concerned, for the quantity of heat and light present in the sparks is not equal to that in fire. The *mahā-bhāgavata,* the great devotee, sees oneness in the sense that he sees everything as the energy of the Supreme Lord. Since there is no difference between the energy and the energetic, there is the sense of oneness. Although from the analytical point of view heat and light are different from fire, there is no meaning to the word "fire" without heat and light. In synthesis, therefore, heat, light and fire are the same.

In this *mantra* the words *ekatvam anupaśyataḥ* indicate that one should see the unity of all living entities from the viewpoint of the revealed scriptures. The individual sparks of the supreme whole (the Lord) possess almost eighty percent of the known qualities of the whole, but they are not quantitatively equal to the Supreme Lord. These qualities are present in minute quantity, for the living entity is but a minute part and parcel of the supreme whole. To use another example, the quantity of salt present in a drop is never comparable to the quantity of salt present in the complete ocean, but the salt present in the drop is qualitatively equal in chemical composition to all the salt present in the ocean. If the individual living being were equal to the Supreme Lord both qualitatively and quantitatively, there would be no question of his being under the influence of the material energy. In the previous *mantras* it has already been discussed that no living being—not even the powerful demigods—can surpass the Supreme Being in any respect. Therefore *ekatvam* does not mean that a living being is equal in all respects to the Supreme Lord. It does, however, indicate that in a broader sense there is one interest, just as in a family the interest of all members is one, or in a nation the national interest is one, although there are many different individual citizens. Since the living entities are all members of the same supreme family, their interest and that of the Supreme Being are not different. Every living being is the son of the Supreme Being. As stated in the *Bhagavad-gītā* (7.5), all living creatures throughout the universe—including birds, reptiles, ants, aquatics, trees and so on—are emanations of the marginal potency of the Supreme Lord. Therefore all of them belong to the family of the Supreme Being. There is no clash of interest.

The spiritual entities are meant for enjoyment, as stated in the *Vedānta-sūtra* (1.1.12): *ānanda-mayo 'bhyāsāt.* By nature and constitution, every living being—including the Supreme Lord and each of His parts and parcels—is meant for eternal enjoyment. The living beings who are encaged in the material tabernacle are constantly seeking enjoyment, but they are seeking it on the wrong platform. Apart from the material platform is the spiritual platform, where the Supreme Being enjoys Himself with His innumerable associates. On that platform there is no trace of material qualities, and therefore that platform is called *nirguṇa*. On the *nirguṇa* platform there is never a clash over the object of enjoyment. Here in the material world there is always a clash between different individual beings because here the proper center of enjoyment is missed. The real center of enjoyment is the Supreme Lord, who is the center of the sublime and spiritual *rāsa* dance. We are all meant to join Him and enjoy life with one transcendental interest and without any clash. That is the highest platform of spiritual interest, and as soon as one realizes this perfect form of oneness, there can be no question of illusion (*moha*) or lamentation (*śoka*).

A godless civilization arises from illusion, and the result of such a civilization is lamentation. A godless civilization, such as that sponsored by the modern politicians, is always full of anxieties because it may be crushed at any moment. That is the law of nature. As stated in the *Bhagavad-gītā* (7.14), none but those who surrender at the lotus feet of the Supreme Lord can surpass the stringent laws of nature. Thus if we wish to get rid of all sorts of illusion and anxiety and create unity out of all diverse interests, we must bring God into all our activities.

The results of our activities must be used to serve the interest of the Lord, and not for any other purpose. Only by serving the Lord's interest can we perceive the *ātma-bhūta* interest mentioned herein. The *ātma-bhūta* interest mentioned in this *mantra* and the *brahma-bhūta* interest mentioned in the *Bhagavad-gītā* (18.54) are one and the same. The supreme *ātmā,* or soul, is the Lord Himself, and the minute *ātmā* is the living entity. The supreme *ātmā,* or Paramātmā, alone maintains all the individual minute beings, for the Supreme Lord wants to derive pleasure out of their affection. The father extends himself through his children and maintains them in order to derive pleasure. If the children obey the father's will, family affairs will run smoothly, with one interest and a pleasing atmosphere. The same situation is transcendentally arranged in the absolute family of the Parabrahman, the Supreme Spirit.

The Parabrahman is as much a person as the individual entities. Neither the Lord nor the living entities are impersonal. Such transcendental personalities are full of transcendental bliss, knowledge and life eternal. That is the real position of spiritual existence, and as soon as one is fully cognizant of this transcendental position, he at once surrenders unto the lotus feet of the Supreme Being, Śrī Kṛṣṇa. But such a *mahātmā,* or great soul, is very rarely seen because such transcendental realization is achieved only after many, many births. Once it is attained, however, there is no longer any illusion or lamentation or the miseries of material existence or birth and death, which are all experienced in our present life. That is the information we get from this *mantra* of *Śrī Īśopaniṣad.*

MANTRA EIGHT

स पर्यगाच्छुक्रमकायमव्रणम्
　　अस्नाविरꣳ शुद्धमपापविद्धम् ।
कविर्मनीषी परिभूः स्वयम्भूर्
　　याथातथ्यतोऽर्थान् व्यदधाच्छाश्वतीभ्यः समाभ्यः ॥८॥

sa paryagāc chukram akāyam avraṇam
asnāviraṁ śuddham apāpa-viddham
kavir manīṣī paribhūḥ svayambhūr
yāthātathyato 'rthān vyadadhāc chāśvatībhyaḥ
samābhyaḥ

saḥ—that person; *paryagāt*—must know in fact; *śukram*—the omnipotent; *akāyam*—unembodied; *avraṇam*—without reproach; *asnāviram*—without veins; *śuddham*—antiseptic; *apāpa-viddham*—prophylactic; *kaviḥ*—omniscient; *manīṣī*—philosopher; *paribhūḥ*—the greatest of all; *svayambhūḥ*—self-sufficient; *yāthātathyataḥ*—just in pursuance of; *arthān*—desirables; *vyadadhāt*—awards; *śāśvatībhyaḥ*—immemorial; *samābhyaḥ*—time.

TRANSLATION

Such a person must factually know the greatest of all, the Personality of Godhead, who is unembodied, omniscient, beyond reproach, without veins, pure

and uncontaminated, the self-sufficient philosopher who has been fulfilling everyone's desire since time immemorial.

PURPORT

Here is a description of the transcendental and eternal form of the Absolute Personality of Godhead. The Supreme Lord is not formless. He has His own transcendental form, which is not at all similar to the forms of the mundane world. The forms of the living entities in this world are embodied in material nature, and they work like any material machine. The anatomy of a material body must have a mechanical construction with veins and so forth, but the transcendental body of the Supreme Lord has nothing like veins. It is clearly stated here that He is unembodied, which means that there is no difference between His body and His soul. Nor is He forced to accept a body according to the laws of nature, as we are. In materially conditioned life, the soul is different from the gross embodiment and subtle mind. For the Supreme Lord, however, there is never any such difference between Him and His body and mind. He is the Complete Whole, and His mind, body and He Himself are all one and the same.

In the *Brahma-saṁhitā* (5.1) there is a similar description of the Supreme Lord. He is described there as *sac-cid-ānanda-vigraha,* which means that He is the eternal form fully representing transcendental existence, knowledge and bliss. As such, He does not require a separate body or mind, as we do in material existence. The Vedic literature clearly states that the Lord's transcendental body is completely different from ours; thus He is sometimes described as formless. This means that He has no form like ours and that He is devoid of a form we can conceive of. In the *Brahma-saṁhitā* (5.32) it is further stated that with each and every part of His body He can do the work of the other senses. This means that the Lord can walk with His hands, accept things with His legs, see with His hands and feet, eat with His eyes, etc. In the *śruti-mantras* it is also said that although the Lord has no hands and legs like ours, He has a different type of hands and legs, by which He can accept all that we offer Him and run faster than anyone. These points are confirmed in this eighth *mantra* through the use of words like *śukram* ("omnipotent").

The Lord's worshipable form (*arcā-vigraha*), which is installed in temples by authorized *ācāryas* who have realized the Lord in terms of Mantra Seven, is nondifferent from the original form of the Lord. The Lord's original form is that of Śrī Kṛṣṇa, and Śrī Kṛṣṇa expands Himself into an unlimited number of forms, such as Baladeva, Rāma, Nṛsiṁha and Varāha. All of these forms are one and the same Personality of Godhead. Similarly, the *arcā-vigraha* worshiped in temples is also an expanded form of the Lord. By worshiping the *arcā-vigraha,* one can at once approach the Lord, who accepts the service of a devotee by His omnipotent energy. The *arcā-vigraha* of the Lord descends at the request of the *ācāryas,* the holy teachers, and works exactly in the original way of the Lord by virtue of the Lord's omnipotence. Foolish people who have no knowledge of *Śrī Īśopaniṣad* or any of the other *śruti-mantras* consider the *arcā-vigraha,* which is worshiped by pure devotees, to be made of material elements. This form may be seen as material by the imperfect eyes of foolish people or *kaniṣṭha-adhikārīs,* but such people do not know that the Lord, being omnipotent and omniscient, can transform matter into spirit and spirit into matter, as He desires.

In the *Bhagavad-gītā* (9.11–12) the Lord regrets the fallen condition of men with little knowledge who deride Him because He descends like a man into this world. Such poorly informed persons do not know the omnipotence of the Lord. Thus the Lord does not manifest Himself in full to the mental speculators. He can be appreciated only in proportion to one's surrender to Him. The fallen condition of the living entities is due entirely to forgetfulness of their relationship with God.

In this *mantra,* as well as in many other Vedic *mantras,* it is clearly stated that the Lord has been supplying goods to the living entities from time immemorial. A living being desires something, and the Lord supplies the object of that desire in proportion to one's qualification. If a man wants to be a high-court judge, he must acquire not only the necessary qualifications but also the consent of the authority who can award the title of high-court judge. The qualifications in themselves are not sufficient for one to occupy the post: it must be awarded by some superior authority. Similarly, the Lord awards enjoyment to living entities in proportion to their qualifications, but good qualifications in themselves are not sufficient to enable one to receive awards. The mercy of the Lord is also required.

Ordinarily the living being does not know what

to ask from the Lord, nor which post to seek. When the living being comes to know his constitutional position, however, he asks to be accepted into the transcendental association of the Lord in order to render transcendental loving service unto Him. Unfortunately, living beings under the influence of material nature ask for many other things, and they are described in the *Bhagavad-gītā* (2.41) as having divided, or splayed, intelligence. Spiritual intelligence is one, but mundane intelligence is diverse. In *Śrīmad-Bhāgavatam* (7.5.30–31) it is stated that those who are captivated by the temporary beauties of the external energy forget the real aim of life, which is to go back to Godhead. Forgetting this, one tries to adjust things by various plans and programs, but this is like chewing what has already been chewed. Nonetheless, the Lord is so kind that He allows the forgetful living entity to continue in this way without interference. Thus this *mantra* of *Śrī Īśopaniṣad* uses the very appropriate word *yāthātathyataḥ,* indicating that the Lord rewards the living entities just in pursuance of their desires. If a living being wants to go to hell, the Lord allows him to do so without interference, and if he wants to go back home, back to Godhead, the Lord helps him.

God is described here as *paribhūḥ,* the greatest of all. No one is greater than or equal to Him. Other living beings are described here as beggars who ask goods from the Lord. The Lord supplies the things the living entities desire. If the entities were equal to the Lord in potency—if they were omnipotent and omniscient—there would be no question of their begging from the Lord, even for so-called liberation. Real liberation means going back to Godhead. Liberation as conceived of by an impersonalist is a myth, and begging for sense gratification has to continue eternally unless the beggar comes to his spiritual senses and realizes his constitutional position.

Only the Supreme Lord is self-sufficient. When Lord Kṛṣṇa appeared on earth five thousand years ago, He displayed His full manifestation as the Personality of Godhead through His various activities. In His childhood He killed many powerful demons, such as Aghāsura, Bakāsura and Śakaṭāsura, and there was no question of His having acquired such power through any extraneous endeavor. He lifted Govardhana Hill without ever practicing weight-lifting. He danced with the *gopīs* without social restriction and without reproach. Although the *gopīs* approached Him with a paramour's feelings of love, the relationship between the *gopīs* and Lord Kṛṣṇa was worshiped even by Lord Caitanya, who was a strict *sannyāsī* and rigid follower of disciplinary regulations. To confirm that the Lord is always pure and uncontaminated, *Śrī Īśopaniṣad* describes Him as *śuddham* (antiseptic) and *apāpa-viddham* (prophylactic). He is antiseptic in the sense that even an impure thing can become purified just by touching Him. The word "prophylactic" refers to the power of His association. As mentioned in the *Bhagavad-gītā* (9.30–31), in the beginning a devotee may appear to be *su-durācāra,* not well-behaved, but he should be accepted as pure because he is on the right path. This is due to the prophylactic nature of the Lord's association. The Lord is also *apāpa-viddham* because sin cannot touch Him. Even if He acts in a way that appears to be sinful, such actions are all-good, for there is no question of His being affected by sin. Because in all circumstances He is *śuddham,* most purified, He is often compared to the sun. The sun extracts moisture from many untouchable places on the earth, yet it remains pure. In fact, it purifies obnoxious things by virtue of its sterilizing powers. If the sun, which is a material object, is so powerful, then we can hardly begin to imagine the purifying strength of the all-powerful Lord.

MANTRA NINE

अन्धं तमः प्रविशन्ति येऽविद्यामुपासते ।
ततो भूय इव ते तमो य उ विद्यायाँ रताः ॥९॥

andhaṁ tamaḥ praviśanti
ye 'vidyām upāsate
tato bhūya iva te tamo
ya u vidyāyāṁ ratāḥ

andham—gross ignorance; *tamaḥ*—darkness; *praviśanti*—enter into; *ye*—those who; *avidyām*—nescience; *upāsate*—worship; *tataḥ*—than that; *bhūyaḥ*—still more; *iva*—like; *te*—they; *tamaḥ*—darkness; *ye*—those who; *u*—also; *vidyāyām*—in the culture of knowledge; *ratāḥ*—engaged.

TRANSLATION

Those who engage in the culture of nescient activities shall enter into the darkest region of ignorance. Worse still are those engaged in the culture of so-called knowledge.

PURPORT

This *mantra* offers a comparative study of *vidyā* and *avidyā. Avidyā,* or ignorance, is undoubtedly dangerous, but *vidyā,* or knowledge, is even more dangerous when mistaken or misguided. This *mantra* of *Śrī Īśopaniṣad* is more applicable today than at any time in the past. Modern civilization has advanced considerably in the field of mass education, but the result is that people are more unhappy than ever before because of the stress placed on material advancement to the exclusion of the most important part of life, the spiritual aspect.

As far as *vidyā* is concerned, the first *mantra* has explained very clearly that the Supreme Lord is the proprietor of everything and that forgetfulness of this fact is ignorance. The more a man forgets this fact of life, the more he is in darkness. In view of this, a godless civilization directed toward the so-called advancement of education is more dangerous than a civilization in which the masses of people are less "educated."

Of the different classes of men—*karmīs, jñānīs* and *yogīs*—the *karmīs* are those who are engaged in the activities of sense gratification. In the modern civilization, 99.9 percent of the people are engaged in the activities of sense gratification under the flags of industrialism, economic development, altruism, political activism, and so on. All these activities are more or less based on satisfaction of the senses, to the exclusion of the kind of God consciousness described in the first *mantra*.

In the language of the *Bhagavad-gītā* (7.15), people who are engaged in gross sense gratification are *mūḍhas*—asses. The ass is a symbol of stupidity. Those who simply engage in the profitless pursuit of sense gratification are worshiping *avidyā,* according to *Śrī Īśopaniṣad.* And those who play the role of helping this sort of civilization in the name of educational advancement are actually doing more harm than those who are on the platform of gross sense gratification. The advancement of learning by a godless people is as dangerous as a valuable jewel on the hood of a cobra. A cobra decorated with a valuable jewel is more dangerous than one not decorated. In the *Hari-bhakti-sudhodaya* (3.11.12), the advancement of education by a godless people is compared to decorations on a dead body. In India, as in many other countries, some people follow the custom of leading a procession with a decorated dead body for the pleasure of the lamenting relatives. In the same way, modern civilization is a patchwork of activities meant to cover the perpetual miseries of material existence. All such activities are aimed toward sense gratification. But above the senses is the mind, and above the mind is the intelligence, and above the intelligence is the soul. Thus the aim of real education should be self-realization, realization of the spiritual values of the soul. Any education which does not lead to such realization must be considered *avidyā,* or nescience. And to culture such nescience means to go down to the darkest region of ignorance.

According to the *Bhagavad-gītā* (2.42, 7.15), mistaken mundane educators are known as *veda-vāda-rata* and *māyayāpahṛta-jñāna*. They may also be atheistic demons, the lowest of men. Those who are *veda-vāda-rata* pose themselves as very learned in the Vedic literature, but unfortunately they are completely diverted from the purpose of the *Vedas.* In the *Bhagavad-gītā* (15.15) it is said that the purpose of the *Vedas* is to know the Personality of Godhead, but these *veda-vāda-rata* men are not at all interested in the Personality of Godhead. On the contrary, they are fascinated by such fruitive results as the attainment of heaven.

As stated in Mantra One, we should know that the Personality of Godhead is the proprietor of everything and that we must be satisfied with our allotted portions of the necessities of life. The purpose of all Vedic literature is to awaken this God consciousness in the forgetful living being, and this same purpose is presented in various ways in the different scriptures of the world for the understanding of a foolish mankind. Thus the ultimate purpose of all religions is to bring one back to Godhead.

But the *veda-vāda-rata* people, instead of realizing that the purpose of the *Vedas* is to revive the forgetful soul's lost relationship with the Personality of Godhead, take it for granted that such side issues as the attainment of heavenly pleasure for sense gratification—the lust for which causes their material bondage in the first place—are the ultimate end of the *Vedas.* Such people misguide others by misinterpreting the Vedic literature. Sometimes they even condemn the *Purāṇas,* which are authentic Vedic explanations for laymen. The *veda-vāda-ratas* give their own explanations of the *Vedas,* neglecting the authority of great teachers (*ācāryas*). They also tend to raise some unscrupulous person from among themselves and present him as the leading exponent of Vedic knowledge. Such *veda-vāda-ratas* are especially condemned in this *mantra* by the very appropriate Sanskrit words *vidyāyāṁ ratāḥ. Vidyāyām* refers to the study of the *Vedas* because the *Vedas* are the origin of all knowledge (*vidyā*), and *ratāḥ* means "those engaged." *Vidyāyāṁ ratāḥ* thus means "those engaged in the study of the *Vedas*." The so-called students of the *Vedas* are condemned herein because they are ignorant of the actual purpose of the *Vedas* on account of their disobeying the *ācāryas*. Such *veda-vāda-ratas* search out meanings in every word of the *Vedas* to suit their own purposes. They do not know that the Vedic literature is a collection of extraordinary books that can be understood only through the chain of disciplic succession.

One must approach a bona fide spiritual master in order to understand the transcendental message of the *Vedas*. That is the direction of the *Muṇḍaka Upaniṣad* (1.2.12). These *veda-vāda-rata* people, however, have their own *ācāryas,* who are not in the chain of transcendental succession. Thus they progress into the darkest region of ignorance by misinterpreting the Vedic literature. They fall even further into ignorance than those who have no knowledge of the *Vedas* at all.

The *māyayāpahṛta-jñāna* class of men are self-made "Gods." Such men think that they themselves are God and that there is no need of worshiping any other God. They will agree to worship an ordinary man if he happens to be rich, but they will never worship the Personality of Godhead. Such men, unable to recognize their own foolishness, never consider how it is that God can be entrapped by *māyā,* His own illusory energy. If God were ever entrapped by *māyā, māyā* would be more powerful than God. Such men say that God is all-powerful, but they do not consider that if He is all-powerful there is no possibility of His being overpowered by *māyā*. These self-made "Gods" cannot answer all these questions very clearly; they are simply satisfied to have become "God" themselves.

MANTRA TEN

अन्यदेवाहुर्विद्ययान्यदाहुरविद्यया ।
इति शुश्रुम धीराणां ये नस्तद्‌ विचचक्षिरे ॥१०॥

anyad evāhur vidyayā-
nyad āhur avidyayā
iti śuśruma dhīrāṇāṁ
ye nas tad vicacakṣire

anyat—different; *eva*—certainly; *āhuḥ*—said; *vidyayā*—by culture of knowledge; *anyat*—different; *āhuḥ*—said; *avidyayā*—by culture of nescience; *iti*—thus; *śuśruma*—I heard; *dhīrāṇām*—from the sober; *ye*—who; *naḥ*—to us; *tat*—that; *vicacakṣire*—explained.

TRANSLATION

The wise have explained that one result is derived from the culture of knowledge and that a different result is obtained from the culture of nescience.

PURPORT

As advised in Chapter Thirteen of the *Bhagavad-gītā* (13.8–12), one should culture knowledge in the following way:

(1) One should become a perfect gentleman and

learn to give proper respect to others.

(2) One should not pose himself as a religionist simply for name and fame.

(3) One should not become a source of anxiety to others by the actions of his body, by the thoughts of his mind, or by his words.

(4) One should learn forbearance even in the face of provocation from others.

(5) One should learn to avoid duplicity in his dealings with others.

(6) One should search out a bona fide spiritual master who can lead him gradually to the stage of spiritual realization, and one must submit himself to such a spiritual master, render him service and ask relevant questions.

(7) In order to approach the platform of self-realization, one must follow the regulative principles enjoined in the revealed scriptures.

(8) One must be fixed in the tenets of the revealed scriptures.

(9) One should completely refrain from practices which are detrimental to the interest of self-realization.

(10) One should not accept more than he requires for the maintenance of the body.

(11) One should not falsely identify himself with the gross material body, nor should one consider those who are related to his body to be his own.

(12) One should always remember that as long as he has a material body he must face the miseries of repeated birth, old age, disease and death. There is no use in making plans to get rid of these miseries of the material body. The best course is to find out the

means by which one may regain his spiritual identity.

(13) One should not be attached to more than the necessities of life required for spiritual advancement.

(14) One should not be more attached to wife, children and home than the revealed scriptures ordain.

(15) One should not be happy or distressed over desirables and undesirables, knowing that such feelings are just created by the mind.

(16) One should become an unalloyed devotee of the Personality of Godhead, Śrī Kṛṣṇa, and serve Him with rapt attention.

(17) One should develop a liking for residence in a secluded place with a calm and quiet atmosphere favorable for spiritual culture, and one should avoid congested places where nondevotees congregate.

(18) One should become a scientist or philosopher and conduct research into spiritual knowledge, recognizing that spiritual knowledge is permanent whereas material knowledge ends with the death of the body.

These eighteen items combine to form a gradual process by which real knowledge can be developed. Except for these, all other methods are considered to be in the category of nescience. Śrīla Bhaktivinoda Ṭhākura, a great *ācārya,* maintained that all forms of material knowledge are merely external features of the illusory energy and that by culturing them one becomes no better than an ass. This same principle is found here in *Śrī Īśopaniṣad.* By advancement of material knowledge, modern man is simply being converted into an ass. Some materialistic politicians in spiritual guise decry the present system of civilization as satanic, but unfortunately they do not care about the culture of real knowledge as it is described in the *Bhagavad-gītā*. Thus they cannot change the satanic situation.

In the modern society, even a boy thinks himself self-sufficient and pays no respect to elderly men. Due to the wrong type of education being imparted in our universities, boys all over the world are giving their elders headaches. Thus *Śrī Īśopaniṣad* very strongly warns that the culture of nescience is different from that of knowledge. The universities are, so to speak, centers of nescience only; consequently scientists are busy discovering lethal weapons to wipe out the existence of other countries. University students today are not given instructions in the regulative principles of *brahmacarya* (celibate student life), nor do they have any faith in any scriptural injunctions. Religious principles are taught for the sake of name and fame only and not for the sake of practical action. Thus there is animosity not only in social and political fields but in the field of religion as well.

Nationalism has developed in different parts of the world due to the cultivation of nescience by the general people. No one considers that this tiny earth is just a lump of matter floating in immeasurable space along with many other lumps. In comparison to the vastness of space, these material lumps are like dust particles in the air. Because God has kindly made these lumps of matter complete in themselves, they are perfectly equipped with all necessities for floating in space. The drivers of our spaceships may be very proud of their achievements, but they do not consider the supreme driver of these greater, more gigantic spaceships called planets.

There are innumerable suns and innumerable planetary systems also. As infinitesimal parts and parcels of the Supreme Lord, we small creatures are trying to dominate these unlimited planets. Thus we take repeated birth and death and are generally frustrated by old age and disease. The span of human life is scheduled for about a hundred years, although it is gradually decreasing to twenty or thirty years. Thanks to the culture of nescience, befooled men have created their own nations within these planets in order to grasp sense enjoyment more effectively for these few years. Such foolish people draw up various plans to render national demarcations perfectly, a task that is totally impossible. Yet for this purpose each and every nation has become a source of anxiety for others. More than fifty percent of a nation's energy is devoted to defense measures and thus spoiled. No one cares for the cultivation of real knowledge, yet people are falsely proud of being advanced in both material and spiritual knowledge.

Śrī Īśopaniṣad warns us of this faulty type of education, and the *Bhagavad-gītā* gives instructions as to the development of real knowledge. This *mantra* states that the instructions of *vidyā* (knowledge) must be acquired from a *dhīra*. A *dhīra* is one who is not disturbed by material illusion. No one can be undisturbed unless he is perfectly spiritually realized, at which time one neither hankers nor laments for anything. A *dhīra* realizes that the material body and mind he has acquired by chance through material association are but foreign elements; therefore he simply makes the best use of a bad bargain.

The material body and mind are bad bargains for

the spiritual living entity. The living entity has actual functions in the living, spiritual world, but this material world is dead. As long as the living spiritual sparks manipulate the dead lumps of matter, the dead world appears to be a living world. Actually it is the living souls, the parts and parcels of the supreme living being, who move the world. The *dhīras* have come to know all these facts by hearing them from superior authorities and have realized this knowledge by following the regulative principles.

To follow the regulative principles, one must take shelter of a bona fide spiritual master. The transcendental message and regulative principles come down from the spiritual master to the disciple. Such knowledge does not come in the hazardous way of nescient education. One can become a *dhīra* only by submissively hearing from a bona fide spiritual master. Arjuna, for example, became a *dhīra* by submissively hearing from Lord Kṛṣṇa, the Personality of Godhead Himself. Thus the perfect disciple must be like Arjuna, and the spiritual master must be as good as the Lord Himself. This is the process of learning *vidyā* (knowledge) from the *dhīra* (the undisturbed).

An *adhīra* (one who has not undergone the training of a *dhīra*) cannot be an instructive leader. Modern politicians who pose themselves as *dhīras* are actually *adhīras,* and one cannot expect perfect knowledge from them. They are simply busy seeing to their own remuneration in dollars and cents. How, then, can they lead the mass of people to the right path of self-realization? Thus one must hear submissively from a *dhīra* in order to attain actual education.

MANTRA ELEVEN

विद्यां चाविद्यां च यस्तद् वेदोभयꣳ सह ।
अविद्यया मृत्युं तीर्त्वा विद्ययामृतमश्नुते ॥११॥

vidyāṁ cāvidyāṁ ca yas
tad vedobhayaṁ saha
avidyayā mṛtyuṁ tīrtvā
vidyayāmṛtam aśnute

vidyām—knowledge in fact; *ca*—and; *avidyām*—nescience; *ca*—and; *yaḥ*—a person who; *tat*—that; *veda*—knows; *ubhayam*—both; *saha*—simultaneously; *avidyayā*—by culture of nescience; *mṛtyum*—repeated death; *tīrtvā*—transcending; *vidyayā*—by culture of knowledge; *amṛtam*—deathlessness; *aśnute*—enjoys.

TRANSLATION

Only one who can learn the process of nescience and that of transcendental knowledge side by side can transcend the influence of repeated birth and death and enjoy the full blessings of immortality.

PURPORT

Since the creation of the material world, everyone has been trying to attain a permanent life, but the laws of nature are so cruel that no one has been able to avoid the hand of death. No one wants to die, nor does anyone want to become old or diseased. The laws of nature, however, do not allow anyone immunity from old age, disease or death. Nor has the advancement of material knowledge solved these problems. Material science can discover the nuclear bomb to accelerate the process of death, but it cannot discover anything that can protect man from the cruel hands of old age, disease and death.

From the *Purāṇas* we learn of the activities of Hiraṇyakaśipu, a king who was very much advanced materially. Wanting to conquer cruel death by his material acquisitions and the strength of his nescience, he underwent a type of meditation so severe that the inhabitants of all the planetary systems became disturbed by his mystic powers. He forced the creator of the universe, the demigod Brahmā, to come down to him. He then asked Brahmā for the benediction of becoming *amara,* by which one does not die. Brahmā said that he could not award the benediction because even he, the material creator who rules all planets, is not *amara.* As confirmed in the *Bhagavad-gītā* (8.17), Brahmā lives a long time, but that does not mean he is immortal.

Hiraṇya means "gold," and *kaśipu* means "soft bed." This cunning gentleman Hiraṇyakaśipu was interested in these two things—money and women—and he wanted to enjoy them by becoming immortal. He asked from Brahmā many benedictions in hopes of indirectly fulfilling his desire to become immortal. Since Brahmā told him that he could not grant the gift of immortality, Hiraṇyakaśipu requested that he not be killed by any man, animal, god or any other living being within the 8,400,000 species. He also asked that he not die on land, in the air or water, or by any weapon. In this way Hiraṇya-kaśipu foolishly thought these guarantees would save him from death. Ultimately, however, although Brahmā granted him all these benedictions, he was killed by the Personality of Godhead in the form of Nṛsiṁha, the Lord's half-lion, half-man incarnation, and no weapon was used to kill him, for he was killed by the Lord's nails. Nor was he killed on the land, in the air or in the water, for he was killed on the lap of that wonderful living being, Nṛsiṁha, who was beyond his conception.

The whole point here is that even Hiraṇyakaśipu, the most powerful of materialists, could not become deathless by his various plans. What, then, can be accomplished by the tiny Hiraṇyakaśipus of today, whose plans are thwarted from moment to moment?

Śrī Īśopaniṣad instructs us not to make one-sided attempts to win the struggle for existence. Everyone is struggling hard for existence, but the laws of material nature are so hard and fast that they do not allow anyone to surpass them. In order to attain a permanent life, one must be prepared to go back to Godhead.

The process by which one goes back to Godhead is a different branch of knowledge, and it has to be learned from revealed Vedic scriptures such as the *Upaniṣads, Vedānta-sūtra, Bhagavad-gītā* and *Śrīmad-Bhāgavatam.* To become happy in this life and attain a permanent blissful life after leaving this material body, one must study this sacred literature and obtain transcendental knowledge. The conditioned living being has forgotten his eternal relationship with God and has mistakenly accepted the temporary place of his birth as all in all. The Lord has kindly delivered the above-mentioned scriptures in India and other scriptures in other countries to remind the forgetful human being that his home is not here in this material world. The living being is a spiritual entity, and he can be happy only by returning to his spiritual home.

From His kingdom the Personality of Godhead sends His bona fide servants to propagate this message by which one can return to Godhead, and sometimes the Lord comes Himself to do this work. Since all living beings are His beloved sons, His parts and parcels, God is more sorry than we ourselves to see the sufferings we are constantly undergoing in this material condition. The miseries of this material world serve to indirectly remind us of our incompatibility with dead matter. Intelligent living entities generally take note of these reminders and engage themselves in the culture of *vidyā,* or transcendental knowledge. Human life is the best opportunity for the culture of spiritual knowledge, and a human being who does not take advantage of this opportunity is called a *narādhama,* the lowest of human beings.

The path of *avidyā,* or advancement of material knowledge for sense gratification, is the path of repeated birth and death. As he exists spiritually, the living entity has no birth or death. Birth and death apply to the outward covering of the spirit soul, the body. Death is compared to the taking off and birth to the putting on of outward garments. Foolish human beings who are grossly absorbed in the culture of *avidyā,* nescience, do not mind this cruel process. Enamored with the beauty of the illusory energy, they undergo the same miseries repeatedly and do not learn any lessons from the laws of nature.

Therefore the culture of *vidyā,* or transcendental knowledge, is essential for the human being. Sense enjoyment in the diseased material condition must be restricted as far as possible. Unrestricted sense enjoyment in this bodily condition is the path of ignorance and death. The living entities are not without spiritual senses; every living being in his original, spiritual form has all the senses, which are now materially manifested, being covered by the material body and mind. The activities of the material senses are perverted reflections of the activities of the original, spiritual senses. In his diseased condition, the spirit soul engages in material activities under the material covering. Real sense enjoyment is possible only when the disease of materialism is removed. In our pure spiritual form, free from all material contamination, real enjoyment of the senses is possible. A patient must regain his health before he can truly enjoy sense pleasure again. Thus the aim of human life should not be to enjoy perverted sense enjoyment but to cure the material disease. Aggravation of the material disease is no sign of knowledge, but a sign of *avidyā,* ignorance. For good health, a person should not increase his fever from 105 degrees to 107 degrees but should reduce his temperature to the normal 98.6. That should be the aim of human life. The modern trend of material civilization is to increase the temperature of the feverish material condition, which has reached the point of 107 degrees in the form of atomic energy. Meanwhile, the foolish politicians are crying that at any moment the world may go to hell. That is the result of the advancement of material knowledge and the neglect of the most important part of life, the culture of spiritual knowledge. *Śrī Īśopaniṣad* herein warns that we must not follow this dangerous path leading to death. On the contrary, we must develop the culture of spiritual knowledge so that we may become completely free from the cruel hands of death.

This does not mean that all activities for the maintenance of the body should be stopped. There is no question of stopping activities, just as there is no question of wiping out one's temperature altogether when trying to recover from a disease. "To make the best use of a bad bargain" is the appropriate expression. The culture of spiritual knowledge necessitates the help of the body and mind; therefore maintenance of the body and mind is required if we are to reach our goal. The normal temperature should be maintained at 98.6 degrees, and the great sages and saints of India have attempted to do this by a balanced program of spiritual and material knowledge. They never allow the misuse of human intelligence for diseased sense gratification.

Human activities diseased by a tendency toward sense gratification have been regulated in the *Vedas* under the principles of salvation. This system employs religion, economic development, sense gratification and salvation, but at the present moment people have no interest in religion or salvation. They have only one aim in life—sense gratification—and in order to achieve this end they make plans for economic development. Misguided men think that religion should be maintained because it contributes to economic development, which is required for sense gratification. Thus in order to guarantee further sense gratification after death, in heaven, there is some system of religious observance. But this is not the purpose of religion. The path of religion is actually meant for self-realization, and economic development is required just to maintain the body in a sound, healthy condition. A man should lead a healthy life with a sound mind just to realize *vidyā,* true knowledge, which is the aim of human life. This life is not meant for working like an ass or for culturing *avidyā* for sense gratification.

The path of *vidyā* is most perfectly presented in *Śrīmad-Bhāgavatam,* which directs a human being to utilize his life to inquire into the Absolute Truth. The Absolute Truth is realized step by step as Brahman, Paramātmā and finally Bhagavān, the Personality of Godhead. The Absolute Truth is realized by the broadminded man who has attained knowledge and detachment by following the eighteen principles of the *Bhagavad-gītā* described in the purport to Mantra Ten. The central purpose of these eighteen principles is the attainment of transcendental devotional service to the Personality of Godhead. Therefore all classes of men are encouraged to learn the art of devotional service to the Lord.

The guaranteed path to the aim of *vidyā* is described by Śrīla Rūpa Gosvāmī in his *Bhakti-rasāmṛta-sindhu,* which we have presented in English as *The Nectar of Devotion.* The culture of *vidyā* is summarized in *Śrīmad-Bhāgavatam*

(1.2.14) in the following words:

tasmād ekena manasā
bhagavān sātvatāṁ patiḥ
śrotavyaḥ kīrtitavyaś ca
dhyeyaḥ pūjyaś ca nityadā

"Therefore, with one-pointed attention one should constantly hear about, glorify, remember and worship the Personality of Godhead, who is the protector of the devotees."

Unless religion, economic development and sense gratification aim toward the attainment of devotional service to the Lord, they are all simply different forms of nescience, as *Śrī Īśopaniṣad* indicates in the following *mantras.*

MANTRA TWELVE

अन्धं तमः प्रविशन्ति येऽसम्भूतिमुपासते ।
ततो भूय इव ते तमो य उ सम्भूत्याँ रताः ॥१२॥

andhaṁ tamaḥ praviśanti
ye 'sambhūtim upāsate
tato bhūya iva te tamo
ya u sambhūtyām̐ ratāḥ

andham—ignorance; *tamaḥ*—darkness; *praviśanti*—enter into; *ye*—those who; *asambhūtim*—demigods; *upāsate*—worship; *tataḥ*—than that; *bhūyaḥ*—still more; *iva*—like that; *te*—those; *tamaḥ*—darkness; *ye*—who; *u*—also; *sambhūtyām*—in the Absolute; *ratāḥ*—engaged.

TRANSLATION

Those who are engaged in the worship of demigods enter into the darkest region of ignorance, and still more so do the worshipers of the impersonal Absolute.

PURPORT

The Sanskrit word *asambhūti* refers to those who have no independent existence. *Sambhūti* is the Absolute Personality of Godhead, who is absolutely independent of everything. In the *Bhagavad-gītā* (10.2), the Absolute Personality of Godhead, Śrī Kṛṣṇa, states:

na me viduḥ sura-gaṇā
prabhavaṁ na maharṣayaḥ
aham ādir hi devānāṁ
maharṣīṇāṁ ca sarvaśaḥ

"Neither the hosts of demigods nor the great sages know My origin or opulences, for in every respect I am the source of the demigods and sages." Thus Kṛṣṇa is the origin of the powers delegated to the demigods, great sages and mystics. Although they are endowed with great powers, these powers are limited, and thus it is very difficult for them to know how Kṛṣṇa Himself appears by His own internal potency in the form of a man.

Many philosophers and great *ṛṣis,* or mystics, try to distinguish the Absolute from the relative by their tiny brain power. This can only help them reach the negative conception of the Absolute without realizing any positive trace of the Absolute. Definition of the Absolute by negation is not complete. Such negative definitions lead one to create a concept of one's own; thus one imagines that the Absolute must be formless and without qualities. Such negative qualities are simply the reversals of relative, material qualities and are therefore also relative. By conceiving of the Absolute in this way, one can at the utmost reach the impersonal effulgence of God, known as Brahman, but one cannot make further progress to Bhagavān, the Personality of Godhead.

Such mental speculators do not know that the Absolute Personality of Godhead is Kṛṣṇa, that the impersonal Brahman is the glaring effulgence of His transcendental body, or that the Paramātmā, the Supersoul, is His all-pervading plenary representation. Nor do they know that Kṛṣṇa has His eternal form with its transcendental qualities of eternal bliss and knowledge. The dependent demigods and great sages imperfectly consider Him to be a powerful demigod, and they consider the Brahman effulgence to be the Absolute Truth. But the devotees of Kṛṣṇa, by dint of their surrendering unto Him and their unalloyed devotion, can know that He is the Absolute Person and that everything emanates from Him. Such devotees continuously render loving service unto Kṛṣṇa, the fountainhead of everything.

In the *Bhagavad-gītā* (7.20, 23) it is said that only unintelligent, bewildered persons driven by a strong desire for sense gratification worship the demigods for the temporary relief of temporary problems. Since the living being is materially entangled, he has to be relieved from material bondage entirely to attain permanent relief on the spiritual plane, where eternal bliss, life and knowledge exist. *Śrī Īśopaniṣad* therefore instructs that we should not seek temporary relief of our difficulties by worshiping the dependent demigods, who can bestow only temporary benefit. Rather, we must worship the Absolute Personality of Godhead, Kṛṣṇa, who is all-attractive and who can bestow upon us complete freedom from material bondage by taking us back home, back to Godhead.

It is stated in the *Bhagavad-gītā* (7.23) that the

worshipers of the demigods can go to the planets of the demigods. The moon worshipers can go to the moon, the sun worshipers to the sun, etc. Modern scientists are now venturing to the moon with the help of rockets, but this is not really a new attempt. With their advanced consciousness, human beings are naturally inclined to travel in outer space and to reach other planets, either by spaceships, mystic powers or demigod worship. In the Vedic scriptures it is said that one can reach other planets by any one of these three ways, but the most common way is by worshiping the demigod presiding over a particular planet. In this way one can reach the moon planet, the sun planet and even Brahmaloka, the topmost planet in this universe. However, all planets in the material universe are temporary residences; the only permanent planets are the Vaikuṇṭhalokas. These are found in the spiritual sky, where the Personality of Godhead Himself predominates. As Lord Kṛṣṇa states in the *Bhagavad-gītā* (8.16):

ā-brahma-bhuvanāl lokāḥ
punar āvartino 'rjuna
mām upetya tu kaunteya
punar janma na vidyate

"From the highest planet in the material world down to the lowest, all are places of misery wherein repeated birth and death take place. But one who attains My abode, O son of Kuntī, never takes birth again."

Śrī Īśopaniṣad points out that one who worships the demigods and attains to their material planets still remains in the darkest region of the universe. The whole universe is covered by the gigantic material elements; it is just like a coconut covered by a shell and half-filled with water. Since its covering is airtight, the darkness within is dense, and therefore the sun and the moon are required for illumination. Outside the universe is the vast and unlimited *brahma-jyoti* expansion, which is filled with Vaikuṇṭhalokas. The biggest and highest planet in the *brahma-jyoti* is Kṛṣṇaloka, or Goloka Vṛndāvana, where the Supreme Personality of Godhead, Śrī Kṛṣṇa Himself, resides. Lord Śrī Kṛṣṇa never leaves Kṛṣṇaloka. Although He dwells there with His eternal associates, He is omnipresent throughout the complete material and spiritual cosmic manifestations. This fact has already been explained in Mantra Four. The Lord is present everywhere, just like the sun, yet He is situated in one place, just as the sun is situated in its own undeviating orbit.

The problems of life cannot be solved simply by going to the moon planet or to some other planet above or below it. Therefore *Śrī Īśopaniṣad* advises us not to bother with any destination within this dark material universe, but to try to get out of it and reach the effulgent kingdom of God. There are many pseudo-worshipers who become religionists only for the sake of name and fame. Such pseudo-religionists do not wish to get out of this universe and reach the spiritual sky. They only want to maintain the status quo in the material world under the garb of worshiping the Lord. The atheists and impersonalists lead such foolish pseudo-religionists into the darkest regions by preaching the cult of atheism. The atheists directly deny the existence of the Supreme Personality of Godhead, and the impersonalists support the atheists by stressing the impersonal aspect of the Supreme Lord. Thus far we have not come across any *mantra* in *Śrī Īśopaniṣad* in which the Supreme Personality of Godhead is denied. It is said that He can run faster than anyone. Those who are running after other planets are certainly persons, and if the Lord can run faster than all of them, how can He be impersonal? The impersonal conception of the Supreme Lord is another form of ignorance, arising from an imperfect conception of the Absolute Truth.

The ignorant pseudo-religionists and the manufacturers of so-called incarnations who directly violate the Vedic injunctions are liable to enter into the darkest region of the universe because they mislead those who follow them. These impersonalists generally pose themselves as incarnations of God to foolish persons who have no knowledge of Vedic wisdom. If such foolish men have any knowledge at all, it is more dangerous in their hands than ignorance itself. Such impersonalists do not even worship the demigods according to the scriptural recommendations. In the scriptures there are recommendations for worshiping demigods under certain circumstances, but at the same time these scriptures state that there is normally no need for this. In the *Bhagavad-gītā* (7.23) it is clearly stated that the results derived from worshiping the demigods are not permanent. Since the entire material universe is impermanent, whatever is achieved within the darkness of material existence is also impermanent. The question is how to obtain real and permanent life.

His Divine Grace
A. C. Bhaktivedanta Swami Prabhupāda
Founder-*Ācārya*
of the International Society for Krishna Consciousness

Yogīs who meditate on the Supersoul in the heart can realize that form when they achieve *samādhi,* complete absorption of the mind. But theirs is still only a partial realization of the Absolute Truth. To realize the Absolute in full, one must practice *bhakti-yoga,* Kṛṣṇa consciousness. (p. 14)

As the embodied soul continuously passes, in this body, from childhood to youth to old age, the soul similarly passes into another body at death. The purpose of human life is to stop this painful process. (pp. 30–31)

I worship Govinda, the primeval Lord, the first progenitor, who is tending the cows fulfilling all desires in abodes filled with spiritual gems and surrounded by millions of wish-fulfilling trees. He is always served with great reverence and affection by hundreds of thousands of Lakṣmīs, or goddesses of fortune. (pp. 118)

The Lord states that as soon as one reaches Him by devotional service—which is the one and only way to approach the Personality of Godhead—one attains complete freedom from the bondage of birth and death. In other words, the path of salvation from the material clutches fully depends on the principles of knowledge and detachment gained from serving the Lord. The pseudo-religionists have neither knowledge nor detachment from material affairs, for most of them want to live in the golden shackles of material bondage under the shadow of philanthropic activities disguised as religious principles. By a false display of religious sentiments, they present a show of devotional service while indulging in all sorts of immoral activities. In this way they pass as spiritual masters and devotees of God. Such violators of religious principles have no respect for the authoritative *ācāryas,* the holy teachers in the strict disciplic succession. They ignore the Vedic injunction *ācāryopāsana*—"One must worship the *ācārya*"—and Kṛṣṇa's statement in the *Bhagavad-gītā* (4.2) *evaṁ paramparā-prāptam,* "This supreme science of God is received through the disciplic succession." Instead, to mislead the people in general they themselves become so-called *ācāryas,* but they do not even follow the principles of the *ācāryas.*

These rogues are the most dangerous elements in human society. Because there is no religious government, they escape punishment by the law of the state. They cannot, however, escape the law of the Supreme, who has clearly declared in the *Bhagavad-gītā* that envious demons in the garb of religious propagandists shall be thrown into the darkest regions of hell (Bg.

16.19–20). *Śrī Īśopaniṣad* confirms that these pseudo-religionists are heading toward the most obnoxious place in the universe after the completion of their spiritual master business, which they conduct simply for sense gratification.

MANTRA THIRTEEN

अन्यदेवाहुः सम्भवादन्यदाहुरसम्भवात् ।
इति शुश्रुम धीराणां ये नस्तद् विचचक्षिरे ॥१३॥

anyad evāhuḥ sambhavād
anyad āhur asambhavāt
iti śuśruma dhīrāṇāṁ
ye nas tad vicacakṣire

anyat—different; *eva*—certainly; *āhuḥ*—it is said; *sambhavāt*—by worshiping the Supreme Lord, the cause of all causes; *anyat*—different; *āhuḥ*—it is said; *asambhavāt*—by worshiping what is not the Supreme; *iti*—thus; *śuśruma*—I heard it; *dhīrāṇām*—from the undisturbed authorities; *ye*—who; *naḥ*—unto us; *tat*—about that subject matter; *vicacakṣire*—perfectly explained.

TRANSLATION

It is said that one result is obtained by worshiping the supreme cause of all causes and that another result is obtained by worshiping what is not supreme. All this is heard from the undisturbed authorities, who clearly explained it.

PURPORT

The system of hearing from undisturbed authorities

is approved in this *mantra.* Unless one hears from a bona fide *ācārya,* who is never disturbed by the changes of the material world, one cannot have the real key to transcendental knowledge. The bona fide spiritual master, who has also heard the *śruti-mantras,* or Vedic knowledge, from his undisturbed *ācārya,* never presents anything that is not mentioned in the Vedic literature. In the *Bhagavad-gītā* (9.25) it is clearly said that those who worship the *pitṛs,* or forefathers, attain the planets of the forefathers, that the gross materialists who make plans to remain here stay in this world, and that the devotees of the Lord who worship none but Lord Kṛṣṇa, the supreme cause of all causes, reach Him in His spiritual sky. Here also in *Śrī Īśopaniṣad* it is verified that one achieves different results by different modes of worship. If we worship the Supreme Lord, we will certainly reach Him in His eternal abode, and if we worship demigods like the sun-god or moon-god, we can reach their respective planets without a doubt. And if we wish to remain on this wretched planet with our planning commissions and our stopgap political adjustments, we can certainly do that also.

Nowhere in authentic scriptures is it said that one will ultimately reach the same goal by doing anything or worshiping anyone. Such foolish theories are offered by self-made "spiritual masters" who have no connection with the *paramparā,* the bona fide system of disciplic succession. The bona fide spiritual master cannot say that all paths lead to the same goal and that anyone can attain this goal by his own mode of worship of the demigods or of the Supreme or whatever. Any common man can very easily understand that a person can reach his destination only when he has purchased a ticket for that destination. A person who has purchased a ticket for Calcutta can reach Calcutta, but not Bombay. But the so-called spiritual masters say that any and all paths will take one to the supreme goal. Such mundane and compromising offers attract many foolish creatures, who become puffed up with their manufactured methods of spiritual realization. The Vedic instructions, however, do not uphold them. Unless one has received knowledge from the bona fide spiritual master who is in the recognized line of disciplic succession, one cannot have the real thing as it is. Kṛṣṇa tells Arjuna in the *Bhagavad-gītā* (4.2):

evaṁ paramparā-prāptam
imaṁ rājarṣayo viduḥ
sa kāleneha mahatā
yogo naṣṭaḥ parantapa

"This supreme science was thus received through the chain of disciplic succession, and the saintly kings understood it in that way. But in course of time the succession was broken, and therefore the science as it is appears to be lost."

When Lord Śrī Kṛṣṇa was present on this earth, the *bhakti-yoga* principles defined in the *Bhagavad-gītā* had become distorted; therefore the Lord had to reestablish the disciplic system beginning with Arjuna, who was the most confidential friend and devotee of the Lord. The Lord clearly told Arjuna (Bg. 4.3) that it was because Arjuna was His devotee and friend that he could understand the principles of the *Bhagavad-gītā*. In other words, only the Lord's devotee and friend can understand the *Gītā*. This also means that only one who follows the path of Arjuna can understand the *Bhagavad-gītā*.

At the present moment there are many interpreters and translators of this sublime dialogue who care nothing for Lord Kṛṣṇa or Arjuna. Such interpreters explain the verses of the *Bhagavad-gītā* in their own way and postulate all sorts of rubbish in the name of the *Gītā*. Such interpreters believe neither in Śrī Kṛṣṇa nor in His eternal abode. How, then, can they explain the *Bhagavad-gītā*?

Kṛṣṇa clearly says that only those who have lost their sense worship the demigods for paltry rewards (Bg. 7.20, 23). Ultimately He advises that one give up all other ways and modes of worship and fully surrender unto Him alone (Bg. 18.66). Only those who are cleansed of all sinful reactions can have such unflinching faith in the Supreme Lord. Others will continue hovering on the material platform with their paltry ways of worship and thus will be misled from the real path under the false impression that all paths lead to the same goal.

In this *mantra* of *Śrī Īśopaniṣad* the word *sambhavāt,* "by worship of the supreme cause," is very significant. Lord Kṛṣṇa is the original Personality of Godhead, and everything that exists has emanated from Him. In the *Bhagavad-gītā* (10.8) the Lord says,

ahaṁ sarvasya prabhavo
mattaḥ sarvaṁ pravartate
iti matvā bhajante māṁ
budhā bhāva-samanvitāḥ

"I am the source of all spiritual and material worlds. Everything emanates from Me. The wise who perfectly know this engage in My devotional service and worship Me with all their hearts."

Here is a correct description of the Supreme Lord, given by the Lord Himself. The words *sarvasya prabhavaḥ* indicate that Kṛṣṇa is the creator of everyone, including Brahmā, Viṣṇu and Śiva. And because these three principal deities of the material world are created by the Lord, the Lord is the creator of all that exists in the material and spiritual worlds. In the *Atharva Veda* (*Gopāla-tāpanī Upaniṣad* 1.24) it is similarly said, "He who existed before the creation of Brahmā and who enlightened Brahmā with Vedic knowledge is Lord Śrī Kṛṣṇa." Similarly, the *Nārāyaṇa Upaniṣad* (1) states, "Then the Supreme Person, Nārāyaṇa, desired to create all living beings. Thus from Nārāyaṇa, Brahmā was born. Nārāyaṇa created all the Prajāpatis. Nārāyaṇa created Indra. Nārāyaṇa created the eight Vasus. Nārāyaṇa created the eleven Rudras. Nārāyaṇa created the twelve Ādityas." Since Nārāyaṇa is a plenary manifestation of Lord Kṛṣṇa, Nārāyaṇa and Kṛṣṇa are one and the same. The *Nārāyaṇa Upaniṣad* (4) also states, "Devakī's son [Kṛṣṇa] is the Supreme Lord." The identity of Nārāyaṇa with the supreme cause has also been accepted and confirmed by Śrīpāda Śaṅkarācārya, even though Śaṅkara does not belong to the Vaiṣṇava, or personalist, cult. The *Atharva Veda* (*Mahā Upaniṣad* 1.2) also states, "Only Nārāyaṇa existed in the beginning, when neither Brahmā, nor Śiva, nor fire, nor water, nor stars, nor sun, nor moon existed. The Lord does not remain alone but creates as He desires." Kṛṣṇa

Himself states in the *Mokṣa-dharma,* "I created the Prajāpatis and the Rudras. They do not have complete knowledge of Me because they are covered by My illusory energy." It is also stated in the *Varāha Purāṇa:* "Nārāyaṇa is the Supreme Personality of Godhead, and from Him the four-headed Brahmā was manifested, as well as Rudra, who later became omniscient."

Thus all Vedic literature confirms that Nārāyaṇa, or Kṛṣṇa, is the cause of all causes. In the *Brahma-saṁhitā* (5.1) also it is said that the Supreme Lord is Śrī Kṛṣṇa, Govinda, the delighter of every living being and the primeval cause of all causes. The really learned persons know this from evidence given by the great sages and the *Vedas,* and thus they decide to worship Lord Kṛṣṇa as all in all. Such persons are called *budha,* or really learned, because they worship only Kṛṣṇa.

The conviction that Kṛṣṇa is all in all is established when one hears the transcendental message from the undisturbed *ācārya* with faith and love. One who has no faith in or love for Lord Kṛṣṇa cannot be convinced of this simple truth. Those who are faithless are described in the *Bhagavad-gītā* (9.11) as *mūḍhas*—fools or asses. It is said that the *mūḍhas* deride the Personality of Godhead because they do not have complete knowledge from the undisturbed *ācārya.* One who is disturbed by the whirlpool of material energy is not qualified to become an *ācārya.*

Before hearing the *Bhagavad-gītā,* Arjuna was disturbed by the material whirlpool, by his affection for his family, society and community. Thus Arjuna wanted to become a philanthropic, nonviolent man of the world. But when he became *budha* by hearing the Vedic knowledge of the *Bhagavad-gītā* from the Supreme Person, he changed his decision and became a worshiper of Lord Śrī Kṛṣṇa, who had Himself arranged the Battle of Kurukṣetra. Arjuna worshiped the Lord by fighting with his so-called relatives, and in this way he became a pure devotee of the Lord. Such accomplishments are possible only when one worships the real Kṛṣṇa and not some fabricated "Kṛṣṇa" invented by foolish men who are without knowledge of the intricacies of the science of Kṛṣṇa described in the *Bhagavad-gītā* and *Śrīmad-Bhāgavatam*.

According to the *Vedānta-sūtra, sambhūta* is the source of birth and sustenance, as well as the reservoir that remains after annihilation (*janmādy asya yataḥ*). The *Śrīmad-Bhāgavatam,* the natural commentary on the *Vedānta-sūtra* by the same author, maintains that the source of all emanations is not like a dead stone but is *abhijña,* or fully conscious. The primeval Lord, Śrī Kṛṣṇa, also says in the *Bhagavad-gītā* (7.26) that He is fully conscious of past, present and future and that no one, including demigods such as Śiva and Brahmā, knows Him fully. Certainly half-educated "spiritual leaders" who are disturbed by the tides of material existence cannot know Him fully. They try to make some compromise by making the mass of humanity the object of worship, but they do not know that such worship is only a myth because the masses are imperfect. The attempt by these so-called spiritual leaders is something like pouring water on the leaves of a tree instead of the root. The natural process is to pour water on the root, but such disturbed leaders are more attracted to the leaves than the root. Despite their perpetually watering the leaves, however, everything dries up for want of nourishment.

Śrī Īśopaniṣad advises us to pour water on the root, the source of all germination. Worship of the mass of humanity by rendering bodily service, which can never be perfect, is less important than service to the soul. The soul is the root that generates different types of bodies according to the law of *karma*. To serve human beings by medical aid, social help and educational facilities while at the same time cutting the throats of poor animals in slaughterhouses is no service at all to the soul, the living being.

The living being is perpetually suffering in different types of bodies from the material miseries of birth, old age, disease and death. The human form of life offers one a chance to get out of this entanglement simply by reestablishing the lost relationship between the living entity and the Supreme Lord. The Lord comes personally to teach this philosophy of surrender unto the Supreme, the *sambhūta*. Real service to humanity is rendered when one teaches surrender to and worship of the Supreme Lord with full love and energy. That is the instruction of *Śrī Īśopaniṣad* in this *mantra*.

The simple way to worship the Supreme Lord in this age of disturbance is to hear and chant about His great activities. The mental speculators, however, think that the activities of the Lord are imaginary; therefore they refrain from hearing of them and invent some word jugglery without any substance to divert the attention of the innocent masses of people. Instead of hearing of the activities of

Lord Kṛṣṇa, such pseudo spiritual masters advertise themselves by inducing their followers to sing about *them*. In modern times the number of such pretenders has increased considerably, and it has become a problem for the pure devotees of the Lord to save the masses of people from the unholy propaganda of these pretenders and pseudo incarnations.

The *Upaniṣads* indirectly draw our attention to the primeval Lord, Śrī Kṛṣṇa, but the *Bhagavad-gītā,* which is the summary of all the *Upaniṣads,* directly points to Śrī Kṛṣṇa. Therefore one should hear about Kṛṣṇa as He is by hearing from the *Bhagavad-gītā* or *Śrīmad-Bhāgavatam,* and in this way one's mind will gradually be cleansed of all contaminated things. *Śrīmad-Bhāgavatam* (1.2.17) says, "By hearing of the activities of the Lord, the devotee draws the attention of the Lord. Thus the Lord, being situated in the heart of every living being, helps the devotee by giving him proper directions." The *Bhagavad-gītā* (10.10) confirms this: *dadāmi buddhi-yogaṁ taṁ yena mām upayānti te.*

The Lord's inner direction cleanses the devotee's heart of all contamination produced by the material modes of passion and ignorance. Nondevotees are under the sway of passion and ignorance. One who is in passion cannot become detached from material hankering, and one who is in ignorance cannot know what he is or what the Lord is. Thus when one is in passion or ignorance, there is no chance for self-realization, however much one may play the part of a religionist. For a devotee, the modes of passion and ignorance are removed by the grace of the Lord. In this way the devotee becomes situated in the quality of goodness, the sign of a perfect *brāhmaṇa*. Anyone can qualify as a *brāhmaṇa* if he follows the path of devotional service under the guidance of a bona fide spiritual master. *Śrīmad-Bhāgavatam* (2.4.18) also says:

kirāta-hūṇāndhra-pulinda-pulkaśā
ābhīra-śumbhā yavanāḥ khasādayaḥ
ye 'nye ca pāpā yad-apāśrayāśrayāḥ
śudhyanti tasmai prabhaviṣṇave namaḥ

Any lowborn person can be purified by the guidance of a pure devotee of the Lord, for the Lord is extraordinarily powerful.

When one attains brahminical qualifications, he becomes happy and enthusiastic to render devotional service to the Lord. Automatically the science of God is unveiled before him. By knowing the science of God, one gradually becomes freed from material attachments, and one's doubtful mind becomes crystal clear by the grace of the Lord. One who attains this stage is a liberated soul and can see the Lord in every step of life. This is the perfection of *sambhava*, as described in this *mantra* of *Śrī Īśopaniṣad*.

MANTRA FOURTEEN

सम्भूतिं च विनाशं च यस्तद् वेदोभयꣳ सह ।
विनाशेन मृत्युं तीर्त्वा सम्भूत्यामृतमश्नुते ॥१४॥

sambhūtiṁ ca vināśaṁ ca
yas tad vedobhayaṁ saha
vināśena mṛtyuṁ tīrtvā
sambhūtyāmṛtam aśnute

sambhūtim—the eternal Personality of Godhead, His transcendental name, form, pastimes, qualities and paraphernalia, the variegatedness of His abode, etc.; *ca*—and; *vināśam*—the temporary material manifestation of demigods, men, animals, etc., with their false names, fame, etc.; *ca*—also; *yaḥ*—one who; *tat*—that; *veda*—knows; *ubhayam*—both; *saha*—along with; *vināśena*—with everything liable to be vanquished; *mṛtyum*—death; *tīrtvā*—surpassing; *sambhūtyā*—in the eternal kingdom of God; *amṛtam*—deathlessness; *aśnute*—enjoys.

TRANSLATION

One should know perfectly the Personality of Godhead Śrī Kṛṣṇa and His transcendental name, form, qualities and pastimes, as well as the temporary material creation with its temporary demigods,

men and animals. When one knows these, he surpasses death and the ephemeral cosmic manifestation with it, and in the eternal kingdom of God he enjoys his eternal life of bliss and knowledge.

PURPORT

By its so-called advancement of knowledge, human civilization has created many material things, including spaceships and atomic energy. Yet it has failed to create a situation in which people need not die, take birth again, become old or suffer from disease. Whenever an intelligent man raises the question of these miseries before a so-called scientist, the scientist very cleverly replies that material science is progressing and that ultimately it will be possible to render man deathless, ageless and diseaseless. Such answers prove the scientists' gross ignorance of material nature. In material nature, everyone is under the stringent laws of matter and must pass through six stages of existence: birth, growth, maintenance, production of by-products, deterioration and finally death. No one in contact with material nature can be beyond these six laws of transformation; therefore no one—whether demigod, man, animal or plant—can survive forever in the material world.

The duration of life varies according to species. Lord Brahmā, the chief living being within this material universe, lives for millions and millions of years, while a minute germ lives for some hours only. But no one in the material world can survive eternally. Things are born or created under certain conditions, they stay for some time, and, if they continue to live, they grow, procreate, gradually dwindle and finally vanish. According to these laws, even the Brahmās, of which there are millions in different universes, are all liable to death either today or tomorrow. Therefore the entire material universe is called Martyaloka, the place of death.

Material scientists and politicians are trying to make this place deathless because they have no information of the deathless spiritual nature. This is due to their ignorance of the Vedic literature, which contains full knowledge confirmed by mature transcendental experience. Unfortunately, modern man is averse to receiving knowledge from the *Vedas, Purāṇas* and other scriptures.

From the *Viṣṇu Purāṇa* (6.7.61) we receive the following information:

viṣṇu-śaktiḥ parā proktā
kṣetra-jñākhyā tathā parā
avidyā-karma-saṁjñānyā
tṛtīyā śaktir iṣyate

Lord Viṣṇu, the Personality of Godhead, possesses different energies, known as *parā* (superior) and *aparā* (inferior). The living entities belong to the superior energy. The material energy, in which we are presently entangled, is the inferior energy. The material creation is made possible by this energy, which covers the living entities with ignorance (*avidyā*) and induces them to perform fruitive activities. Yet there is another part of the Lord's superior energy that is different from both this material, inferior energy and the living entities. That superior energy constitutes the eternal, deathless abode of the Lord. This is confirmed in the *Bhagavad-gītā* (8.20):

paras tasmāt tu bhāvo 'nyo
'vyakto 'vyaktāt sanātanaḥ
yaḥ sa sarveṣu bhūteṣu
naśyatsu na vinaśyati

All the material planets—upper, lower and intermediate, including the sun, moon and Venus—are scattered throughout the universe. These planets exist only during the lifetime of Brahmā. Some lower planets, however, are vanquished after the end of one day of Brahmā and are again created during the next day of Brahmā. On the upper planets, time is calculated differently. One of our years is equal to only twenty-four hours, or one day and night, on many of the upper planets. The four ages of earth (Satya, Tretā, Dvāpara and Kali) last only twelve thousand years according to the time scale of the upper planets. Such a length of time multiplied by one thousand constitutes one day of Brahmā, and one night of Brahmā is the same. Such days and nights accumulate into months and years, and Brahmā lives for one hundred such years. At the end of Brahmā's life, the complete universal manifestation is vanquished.

Those living beings who reside on higher planets like the sun and the moon, as well as those on Martyaloka, this earth planet, and also those who live on lower planets—all are merged into the waters of devastation during the night of Brahmā. During this time no living beings or species remain manifest, although spiritually they continue to exist.

This unmanifested stage is called *avyakta*. Again, when the entire universe is vanquished at the end of Brahmā's lifetime, there is another *avyakta* state. But beyond these two unmanifested states is another unmanifested state, the spiritual atmosphere, or nature. There are a great number of spiritual planets in this atmosphere, and these planets exist eternally, even when all the planets within this material universe are vanquished at the end of Brahmā's life. There are many material universes, each under the jurisdiction of a Brahmā, and this cosmic manifestation within the jurisdiction of the various Brahmās is but a display of one fourth of the energy of the Lord (*ekapād-vibhūti*). This is the inferior energy. Beyond the jurisdiction of Brahmā is the spiritual nature, which is called *tripād-vibhūti,* three fourths of the Lord's energy. This is the superior energy, or *parā-prakṛti.*

The predominating Supreme Person residing within the spiritual nature is Lord Śrī Kṛṣṇa. As confirmed in the *Bhagavad-gītā* (8.22), He can be approached only by unalloyed devotional service and not by the processes of *jñāna* (philosophy), *yoga* (mysticism) or *karma* (fruitive work). The *karmīs,* or fruitive workers, can elevate themselves to the Svargaloka planets, which include the sun and the moon. *Jñānīs* and *yogīs* can attain still higher planets, such as Maharloka, Tapoloka and Brahmaloka, and when they become still more qualified through devotional service they can enter into the spiritual nature, either the illuminating cosmic atmosphere of the spiritual sky (Brahman) or the Vaikuṇṭha planets, according to their qualification. It is certain, however, that no one can enter into the spiritual Vaikuṇṭha planets without being trained in devotional service.

On the material planets, everyone from Brahmā down to the ant is trying to lord it over material nature, and this is the material disease. As long as this material disease continues, the living entity has to undergo the process of bodily change. Whether he takes the form of a man, demigod or animal, he ultimately has to endure an unmanifested condition during the two devastations—the devastation during the night of Brahmā and the devastation at the end of Brahmā's life. If we want to put an end to this process of repeated birth and death, as well as the concomitant factors of old age and disease, we must try to enter the spiritual planets, where we can live eternally in the association of Lord Kṛṣṇa or His plenary expansions, His Nārāyaṇa forms. Lord Kṛṣṇa or His plenary expansions dominate every one of these innumerable planets, a fact confirmed in the *śruti mantras: eko vaśī sarva-gaḥ kṛṣṇa īḍyaḥ/ eko 'pi san bahudhā yo 'vabhāti.* (*Gopāla-tāpanī Upaniṣad* 1.21)

No one can dominate Kṛṣṇa. It is the conditioned soul who tries to dominate material nature and is instead subjected to the laws of material nature and the sufferings of repeated birth and death. The Lord comes here to reestablish the principles of religion, and the basic principle is the development of an attitude of surrender to Him. This is the Lord's last instruction in the *Bhagavad-gītā* (18.66): *sarva-dharmān parityajya mām ekaṁ śaraṇaṁ vraja.* "Give up all other processes and just surrender unto Me alone." Unfortunately, foolish men have misinterpreted this prime teaching and misled the masses of people in diverse ways. People have been urged to open hospitals but not to educate themselves to enter into the spiritual kingdom by devotional service. They have been taught to take interest only in temporary relief work, which can never bring real happiness to the living entity. They start varieties of public and semi-governmental institutions to tackle the devastating power of nature, but they don't know how to pacify insurmountable nature. Many men are advertised as great scholars of the *Bhagavad-gītā,* but they overlook the *Gītā's* message, by which material nature can be pacified. Powerful nature can be pacified only by the awakening of God consciousness, as clearly pointed out in the *Bhagavad-gītā* (7.14).

In this *mantra, Śrī Īśopaniṣad* teaches that one must perfectly know both *sambhūti* (the Personality of Godhead) and *vināśa* (the temporary material manifestation), side by side. By knowing the material manifestation alone, one cannot be saved, for in the course of nature there is devastation at every moment (*ahany ahani bhūtāni gacchantīha yamālayam*). Nor can one be saved from these devastations by the opening of hospitals. One can be saved only by complete knowledge of the eternal life of bliss and awareness. The whole Vedic scheme is meant to educate men in this art of attaining eternal life. People are often misguided by temporary attractive things based on sense gratification, but service rendered to the sense objects is both misleading and degrading.

We must therefore save ourselves and our fellow man in the right way. There is no question of liking or disliking the truth. It is there. If we want to be saved from repeated birth and death, we must take to the devotional service of the Lord. There can be no compromise, for this is a matter of necessity.

MANTRA FIFTEEN

हिरण्मयेन पात्रेण सत्यस्यापिहितं मुखम् ।
तत् त्वं पूषन्नपावृणु सत्यधर्माय दृष्टये ॥१५॥

hiraṇmayena pātreṇa
satyasyāpihitaṁ mukham
tat tvaṁ pūṣann apāvṛṇu
satya-dharmāya dṛṣṭaye

hiraṇmayena—by a golden effulgence; *pātreṇa*—by a dazzling covering; *satyasya*—of the Supreme Truth; *apihitam*—covered; *mukham*—the face; *tat*—that covering; *tvam*—Yourself; *pūṣan*—O sustainer; *apāvṛṇu*—kindly remove; *satya*—pure; *dharmāya*—unto the devotee; *dṛṣṭaye*—for exhibiting.

TRANSLATION

O my Lord, sustainer of all that lives, Your real face is covered by Your dazzling effulgence. Kindly remove that covering and exhibit Yourself to Your pure devotee.

PURPORT

In the *Bhagavad-gītā* (14.27), the Lord explains His personal rays (*brahma-jyoti*), the dazzling effulgence of His personal form, in this way:

brahmaṇo hi pratiṣṭhāham
amṛtasyāvyayasya ca
śāśvatasya ca dharmasya
sukhasyaikāntikasya ca

"I am the basis of the impersonal Brahman, which is immortal, imperishable and eternal and is the constitutional position of ultimate happiness." Brahman, Paramātmā and Bhagavān are three aspects of the same Absolute Truth. Brahman is the aspect most easily perceived by the beginner; Paramātmā, the Supersoul, is realized by those who have further progressed; and Bhagavān realization is the ultimate realization of the Absolute Truth. This is confirmed in the *Bhagavad-gītā* (7.7), where Lord Kṛṣṇa says that He is the ultimate concept of the Absolute Truth: *mattaḥ parataraṁ nānyat.* Therefore Kṛṣṇa is the source of the *brahma-jyoti* as well as the all-pervading Paramātmā. Later in the *Bhagavad-gītā* (10.42) Kṛṣṇa further explains:

atha vā bahunaitena
kiṁ jñātena tavārjuna
viṣṭabhyāham idaṁ kṛtsnam
ekāṁśena sthito jagat

"But what need is there, Arjuna, for all this detailed knowledge? With a single fragment of Myself I pervade and support this entire universe." Thus by His one plenary expansion, the all-pervading Paramātmā, the Lord maintains the complete material cosmic creation. He also maintains all manifestations in the spiritual world. Therefore in this *śruti-mantra* of

Śrī Īśopaniṣad, the Lord is addressed as *pūṣan,* the ultimate maintainer.

The Personality of Godhead, Śrī Kṛṣṇa, is always filled with transcendental bliss (*ānanda-mayo 'bhyāsāt*). When He was present at Vṛndāvana in India five thousand years ago, He always remained in transcendental bliss, even from the beginning of His childhood pastimes. The killings of various demons—such as Agha, Baka, Pūtanā and Pralamba—were but pleasure excursions for Him. In His village of Vṛndāvana He enjoyed Himself with His mother, brother and friends, and when He played the role of a naughty butter thief, all His associates enjoyed celestial bliss by His stealing. The Lord's fame as a butter thief is not reproachable, for by stealing butter the Lord gave pleasure to His pure devotees. Everything the Lord did in Vṛndāvana was for the pleasure of His associates there. The Lord created these pastimes to attract the dry speculators and the acrobats of the so-called *haṭha-yoga* system who wish to find the Absolute Truth.

Of the childhood play between the Lord and His playmates, the cowherd boys, Śukadeva Gosvāmī says in *Śrīmad-Bhāgavatam* (10.12.11):

itthaṁ satāṁ brahma-sukhānubhūtyā
dāsyaṁ gatānāṁ para-daivatena
māyāśritānāṁ nara-dārakeṇa
sākaṁ vijahruḥ kṛta-puṇya-puñjāḥ

"The Personality of Godhead, who is perceived as the impersonal, blissful Brahman by the *jñānīs,* who is worshiped as the Supreme Lord by devotees in the mood of servitorship, and who is considered an ordinary human being by mundane people, played with the cowherd boys, who had attained their position after accumulating many pious activities."

Thus the Lord is always engaged in transcendental loving activities with His spiritual associates in the various relationships of *śānta* (neutrality), *dāsya* (servitorship), *sakhya* (friendship), *vātsalya* (parental affection) and *mādhurya* (conjugal love).

Since it is said that Lord Kṛṣṇa never leaves Vṛndāvana-dhāma, one may ask how He manages the affairs of the creation. This is answered in the *Bhagavad-gītā* (13.14–18): The Lord pervades the entire material creation by His plenary part known as the Paramātmā, or Supersoul. Although the Lord personally has nothing to do with material creation, maintenance and destruction, He causes all these things to be done by His plenary expansion, the Paramātmā. Every living entity is known as *ātmā,* soul, and the principal *ātmā* who controls them all is Paramātmā, the Supersoul.

This system of God realization is a great science. The materialistic *sāṅkhya-yogīs* can only analyze and meditate on the twenty-four factors of the material creation, for they have very little information of the *puruṣa,* the Lord. And the impersonal transcendentalists are simply bewildered by the glaring effulgence of the *brahma-jyoti*. If one wants to see the Absolute Truth in full, one has to penetrate beyond the twenty-four material elements and the glaring effulgence as well. *Śrī Īśopaniṣad* points toward this direction, praying for the removal of the *hiraṇmaya-pātra,* the dazzling covering of the Lord.

Unless this covering is removed so one can perceive the real face of the Personality of Godhead, factual realization of the Absolute Truth can never be achieved.

The Paramātmā feature of the Personality of Godhead is one of three plenary expansions, or *viṣṇu-tattvas,* collectively known as the *puruṣa-avatāras.* One of these *viṣṇu-tattvas* who is within the universe is known as Kṣīrodakaśāyī Viṣṇu. He is Viṣṇu among the three principal deities—Brahmā, Viṣṇu and Śiva—and He is the all-pervading Paramātmā in each and every individual living entity. The second *viṣṇu-tattva* within the universe is Garbhodakaśāyī Viṣṇu, the collective Supersoul of all living entities. Beyond these two is Kāraṇodakaśāyī Viṣṇu, who lies in the Causal Ocean. He is the creator of all universes. The *yoga* system teaches the serious student to meet the *viṣṇu-tattvas* after going beyond the twenty-four material elements of the cosmic creation. The culture of empiric philosophy helps one realize the impersonal *brahma-jyoti,* which is the glaring effulgence of the transcendental body of Lord Śrī Kṛṣṇa. That the *brahma-jyoti* is Kṛṣṇa's effulgence is confirmed in the *Bhagavad-gītā* (14.27) as well as the *Brahma-saṁhitā* (5.40):

yasya prabhā-prabhavato jagad-aṇḍa-koṭi-
koṭiṣv aśeṣa-vasudhādi vibhūti-bhinnam
tad brahma niṣkalam anantam aśeṣa-bhūtaṁ
govindam ādi-puruṣaṁ tam ahaṁ bhajāmi

"In the millions and millions of universes there are innumerable planets, and each and every one of them is different from the others by its cosmic constitution. All of these planets are situated in a corner of the *brahma-jyoti.* This *brahma-jyoti* is but the personal rays of the Supreme Personality of Godhead, Govinda, whom I worship." This *mantra* from the *Brahma-saṁhitā* is spoken from the platform of factual realization of the Absolute Truth, and the *śruti-mantra* of *Śrī Īśopaniṣad* under discussion confirms this *mantra* as a process of realization. The *Īśopaniṣad mantra* is a simple prayer to the Lord to remove the *brahma-jyoti* so that one can see His real face. This *brahma-jyoti* effulgence is described in detail in several *mantras* of the *Muṇḍaka Upaniṣad* (2.2.9–11):

hiraṇmaye pare kośe
virajaṁ brahma niṣkalam
tac chubhraṁ jyotiṣāṁ jyotis
tad yad ātma-vido viduḥ

na tatra sūryo bhāti na candra-tārakaṁ
nemā vidyuto bhānti kuto 'yam agniḥ
tam eva bhāntam anu bhāti sarvaṁ
tasya bhāsā sarvam idaṁ vibhāti

brahmaivedam amṛtaṁ purastād brahma
paścād brahma dakṣiṇataś cottareṇa
adhaś cordhvaṁ ca prasṛtaṁ brahmai-
vedaṁ viśvam idaṁ variṣṭham

"In the spiritual realm, beyond the material covering, is the unlimited Brahman effulgence, which is free from material contamination. That effulgent white light is understood by transcendentalists to be the light of all lights. In that realm there is no need of sunshine, moonshine, fire or electricity for illumination. Indeed, whatever illumination appears in the material world is only a reflection of that supreme illumination. That Brahman is in front and in back, in the north, south, east and west, and also overhead and below. In other words, that supreme Brahman effulgence spreads throughout both the material and spiritual skies."

Perfect knowledge means knowing Kṛṣṇa as the root of this Brahman effulgence. This knowledge can be gained from such scriptures as *Śrīmad-Bhāgavatam,* which perfectly elaborates the science of Kṛṣṇa. In *Śrīmad-Bhāgavatam,* the author, Śrīla Vyāsadeva, has established that one will describe the Supreme Truth as Brahman, Paramātmā or Bhagavān according to one's realization of Him. Śrīla Vyāsadeva never states that the Supreme Truth is a *jīva,* an ordinary living entity. The living entity should never be considered the all-powerful Supreme Truth. If he were the Supreme, he would not need to pray to the Lord to remove His dazzling cover so that the living entity could see His real face.

The conclusion is that one who has no knowledge of the potencies of the Supreme Truth will realize the impersonal Brahman. Similarly, when one realizes the material potencies of the Lord but has little or no information of the spiritual potencies, he attains Paramātmā realization. Thus both Brahman and Paramātmā realization of the Absolute Truth are partial realizations. However, when one realizes the Supreme Personality of Godhead, Śrī Kṛṣṇa, in full potency after the removal of the *hiraṇmaya-pātra,* one realizes *vāsudevaḥ sarvam iti:* Lord Śrī Kṛṣṇa, who is known as Vāsudeva, is everything—Brahman, Paramātmā and Bhagavān. He is Bhagavān, the root, and Brahman and Paramātmā are His branches.

In the *Bhagavad-gītā* (6.46–47) there is a comparative analysis of the three types of transcendentalists—the worshipers of the impersonal Brahman (*jñānīs*), the worshipers of the Paramātmā feature (*yogīs*) and the devotees of Lord Śrī Kṛṣṇa (*bhaktas*). It is stated there that the *jñānīs,* those who have cultivated Vedic knowledge, are better than ordinary fruitive workers, that the *yogīs* are still greater than the *jñānīs,* and that among all *yogīs,* those who constantly serve the Lord with all their energies are the topmost. In summary, a philosopher is better than a laboring man, a mystic is superior to a philosopher, and of all the mystic *yogīs*, he who follows *bhakti-yoga,* constantly engaging in the service of the Lord, is the highest. *Śrī Īśopaniṣad* directs us toward this perfection.

MANTRA SIXTEEN

पूषन्नेकर्षे यम सूर्य प्राजापत्य
व्यूह रश्मीन् समूह ।
तेजो यत् ते रूपं कल्याणतमं
तत् ते पश्यामि योऽसावसौ पुरुषः सोऽहमस्मि ॥१६॥

pūṣann ekarṣe yama sūrya prājāpatya
vyūha raśmīn samūha
tejo yat te rūpaṁ kalyāṇa-tamaṁ
tat te paśyāmi yo 'sāv asau puruṣaḥ so 'ham asmi

pūṣan—O maintainer; *eka-ṛṣe*—the primeval philosopher; *yama*—the regulating principle; *sūrya*—the destination of the *sūris* (great devotees); *prājāpatya*—the well-wisher of the *prajāpatis* (progenitors of mankind); *vyūha*—kindly remove; *raśmīn*—the rays; *samūha*—kindly withdraw; *tejaḥ*—effulgence; *yat*—so that; *te*—Your; *rūpam*—form; *kalyāṇa-tamam*—most auspicious; *tat*—that; *te*—Your; *paśyāmi*—I may see; *yaḥ*—one who is; *asau*—like the sun; *asau*—that; *puruṣaḥ*—Personality of Godhead; *saḥ*—myself; *aham*—I; *asmi*—am.

TRANSLATION

O my Lord, O primeval philosopher, maintainer of the universe, O regulating principle, destination of

the pure devotees, well-wisher of the progenitors of mankind, please remove the effulgence of Your transcendental rays so that I can see Your form of bliss. You are the eternal Supreme Personality of Godhead, like unto the sun, as am I.

PURPORT

The sun and its rays are one and the same qualitatively. Similarly, the Lord and the living entities are one and the same in quality. The sun is one, but the molecules of the sun's rays are innumerable. The sun's rays constitute part of the sun, and the sun and its rays conjointly constitute the complete sun. Within the sun itself resides the sun-god, and similarly within the supreme spiritual planet, Goloka Vṛndāvana, from which the *brahma-jyoti* effulgence is emanating, the Lord enjoys His eternal pastimes, as verified in the *Brahma-saṁhitā* (5.29):

cintāmaṇi-prakara-sadmasu kalpa-vṛkṣa-
lakṣāvṛteṣu surabhīr abhipālayantam
lakṣmī-sahasra-śata-sambhrama-sevyamānaṁ
govindam ādi-puruṣaṁ tam ahaṁ bhajāmi

"I worship Govinda, the primeval Lord, the first progenitor, who is tending the cows fulfilling all desires in abodes filled with spiritual gems and surrounded by millions of wish-fulfilling trees. He is always served with great reverence and affection by hundreds of thousands of Lakṣmīs, or goddesses of fortune."

The *brahma-jyoti* is described in the *Brahma-saṁhitā* as the rays emanating from that supreme spiritual planet, Goloka Vṛndāvana, just as the sun's rays emanate from the sun globe. Until one surpasses the glare of the *brahma-jyoti,* one cannot receive information of the land of the Lord. The impersonalist philosophers, blinded as they are by the dazzling *brahma-jyoti,* can realize neither the factual abode of the Lord nor His transcendental form. Limited by their poor fund of knowledge, such impersonalist thinkers cannot understand the all-blissful transcendental form of Lord Kṛṣṇa. In this prayer, therefore, *Śrī Īśopaniṣad* petitions the Lord to remove the effulgent rays of the *brahma-jyoti* so that the pure devotee can see His all-blissful transcendental form.

By realizing the impersonal *brahma-jyoti,* one experiences the auspicious aspect of the Supreme, and by realizing the Paramātmā, or all-pervading feature of the Supreme, one experiences an even more auspicious enlightenment. But by meeting the Personality of Godhead Himself face to face, the devotee experiences the most auspicious feature of the Supreme. Since He is addressed as the primeval philosopher and maintainer and well-wisher of the universe, the Supreme Truth cannot be impersonal. This is the verdict of *Śrī Īśopaniṣad.* The word *pūṣan* ("maintainer") is especially significant, for although the Lord maintains all beings, He specifically maintains His devotees. After surpassing the impersonal *brahma-jyoti* and seeing the personal aspect of the Lord and His most auspicious eternal form, the devotee realizes the Absolute Truth in full.

In his *Bhagavat-sandarbha,* Śrīla Jīva Gosvāmī states: "The complete conception of the Absolute

Truth is realized in the Personality of Godhead because He is almighty and possesses full transcendental potencies. The full potency of the Absolute Truth is not realized in the *brahma-jyoti;* therefore Brahman realization is only partial realization of the Personality of Godhead. O learned sages, the first syllable of the word *bhagavān* (*bha*) has two meanings: the first is 'one who fully maintains,' and the second is 'guardian.' The second syllable (*ga*) means 'guide,' 'leader' or 'creator.' The syllable *vān* indicates that every being lives in Him and that He also lives in every being. In other words, the transcendental sound *bhagavān* represents infinite knowledge, potency, energy, opulence, strength and influence—all without a tinge of material inebriety."

The Lord fully maintains His unalloyed devotees, and He guides them progressively on the path toward devotional perfection. As the leader of His devotees, He ultimately awards the desired results of devotional service by giving Himself to them. The devotees of the Lord see the Lord eye to eye by His causeless mercy; thus the Lord helps His devotees reach the supermost spiritual planet, Goloka Vṛndāvana. Being the creator, He can bestow all necessary qualifications upon His devotees so that they can ultimately reach Him. The Lord is the cause of all causes. In other words, since there is nothing that caused Him, He is the original cause. Consequently He enjoys His own Self by manifesting His own internal potency. The external potency is not exactly manifested by Him, for He expands Himself as the *puruṣas,* and it is in these forms that He maintains the features of the material manifestation. By such expansions, He creates, maintains and annihilates the cosmic manifestation.

The living entities are also differentiated expansions of the Lord's Self, and because some of them desire to be lords and imitate the Supreme Lord, He allows them to enter into the cosmic creation with the option to fully utilize their propensity to lord it over nature. Because of the presence of His parts and parcels, the living entities, the entire phenomenal world is stirred into action and reaction. Thus the living entities are given full facilities to lord it over material nature, but the ultimate controller is the Lord Himself in His plenary feature as Paramātmā, the Supersoul, who is one of the *puruṣas*.

Thus there is a gulf of difference between the living entity (*ātmā*) and the controlling Lord (Paramātmā), the soul and the Supersoul. Paramātmā is the controller, and the *ātmā* is the controlled; therefore they are in different categories. Because the Paramātmā fully cooperates with the *ātmā,* He is known as the constant companion of the living being.

The all-pervading feature of the Lord—which exists in all circumstances of waking and sleeping as well as in potential states and from which the *jīva-śakti* (living force) is generated as both conditioned and liberated souls—is known as Brahman. Since the Lord is the origin of both Paramātmā and Brahman, He is the origin of all living entities and all else that exists. Those who know this engage at once in the devotional service of the Lord. Such pure and fully cognizant devotees of the Lord are fully attached to Him heart and soul, and whenever such devotees assemble with similar devotees, they have no engagement but the glorification of the Lord's transcendental activities. Those who are not as perfect as the pure devotees—namely, those who have realized only the Brahman or Paramātmā features of the Lord—cannot appreciate the activities of the perfect devotees. The Lord always helps the pure devotees by imparting necessary knowledge within their hearts, and thus out of His special favor He dissipates all the darkness of ignorance. The speculative philosophers and *yogīs* cannot imagine this, because they more or less depend on their own strength. As stated in the *Kaṭha Upaniṣad* (1.2.23), the Lord can be known only by those whom He favors, and not by anyone else. Such special favors are bestowed upon His pure devotees only. *Śrī Īśopaniṣad* thus points to the favor of the Lord, which is beyond the purview of the *brahma-jyoti.*

MANTRA SEVENTEEN

वायुरनिलममृतमथेदं भस्मान्तं शरीरम् ।
ॐ क्रतो स्मर कृतं स्मर क्रतो स्मर कृतं स्मर ॥१७॥

vāyur anilam amṛtam
athedaṁ bhasmāntaṁ śarīram
oṁ krato smara kṛtaṁ smara
krato smara kṛtaṁ smara

vāyuḥ—air of life; *anilam*—total reservoir of air; *amṛtam*—indestructible; *atha*—now; *idam*—this; *bhasmāntam*—after being turned into ashes; *śarīram*—body; *oṁ*—O Lord; *krato*—O enjoyer of all sacrifices; *smara*—please remember; *kṛtam*—all that has been done by me; *smara*—please remember; *krato*—O supreme beneficiary; *smara*—please remember; *kṛtam*—all that I have done for You; *smara*—please remember.

TRANSLATION

Let this temporary body be burnt to ashes, and let the air of life be merged with the totality of air. Now, O my Lord, please remember all my sacrifices, and because You are the ultimate beneficiary, please remember all that I have done for You.

PURPORT

The temporary material body is certainly a foreign dress. The *Bhagavad-gītā* (2.20) clearly says that after the destruction of the material body the living entity is not annihilated, nor does he lose his identity. The identity of the living entity is never impersonal or formless; on the contrary, it is the material dress that is formless and that takes a shape according to the form of the indestructible person. No living entity is originally formless, as is wrongly thought by those with a poor fund of knowledge. This *mantra* verifies the fact that the living entity exists after the annihilation of the material body.

In the material world, material nature displays wonderful workmanship by creating varieties of bodies for the living beings according to their propensities for sense gratification. The living entity who wants to taste stool is given a material body that is quite suitable for eating stool—that of a hog. Similarly, one who wants to eat the flesh and blood of other animals may be given a tiger's body equipped with suitable teeth and claws. But the human being is not meant for eating flesh, nor does he have any desire to taste stool, even in the most aboriginal state. Human teeth are so made that they can chew and cut fruit and vegetables, although there are two canine teeth so that primitive humans can eat flesh if they so desire.

But in any case, the material bodies of all animals and men are foreign to the living entity. They change according to the living entity's desire for sense gratification. In the cycle of evolution, the living entity changes bodies one after another. When the world was full of water, the living entity took an aquatic form. Then he passed to vegetable life, from vegetable life to worm life, from worm life to bird life, from bird life to animal life, and from animal life to the human form. The highest developed form is this human form when it is possessed of a full sense of spiritual knowledge. The highest development of one's spiritual sense is described in this *mantra:* One should give up the material body, which will be turned to ashes, and allow the air of life to merge into the eternal reservoir of air. The living being's activities are performed within the body through the movements of different kinds of air, known in summary as *prāṇa-vāyu.* The *yogīs* generally study how to control the airs of the body. The soul is supposed to rise from one circle of air to another until it rises to the *brahma-randhra,* the highest circle. From that point the perfect *yogī* can transfer himself to any planet he likes. The process is to give up one material body and then enter into another. But the highest perfection of such changes occurs only when the living entity is able to give up the material body altogether, as suggested in this *mantra,* and enter into the spiritual atmosphere, where he can develop a completely different type of body—a spiritual body, which never has to meet death or change.

Here in the material world, material nature forces the living entity to change his body due to his different desires for sense gratification. These desires are represented in the various species of life, from germs to the most perfected material bodies, those of Brahmā and the demigods. All of these living entities have bodies composed of matter in different shapes. The intelligent man sees oneness not in the variety of the bodies but in the spiritual identity. The spiritual spark, which is part and parcel of the Supreme Lord, is the same whether he is in a body of a hog or in the body of a demigod. The living entity takes on different bodies according to his pious and vicious activities. The human body is highly developed and has full consciousness. According to the *Bhagavad-gītā* (7.19), the most perfect man surrenders unto the Lord after many, many lifetimes of culturing knowledge. The culture of knowledge reaches perfection only when the knower comes to the point of surrendering unto the Supreme Lord, Vāsudeva. Otherwise, even after attaining knowledge of one's spiritual identity, if one does not come to the point of knowing that the living entities are eternal parts and parcels of the whole and can never become the whole, one has to fall down again into the material atmosphere. Indeed, one must fall down even if he has become one with the *brahma-jyoti.*

As we have learned from previous *mantras,* the *brahma-jyoti* emanating from the transcendental body of the Lord is full of spiritual sparks that are individual entities with the full sense of existence. Sometimes these living entities want to enjoy their senses, and therefore they are placed in the material world to become false lords under the dictation of the senses. The desire for lordship is the material disease of the living being, for under the spell of sense enjoyment he transmigrates through the various bodies manifested in the material world. Becoming one with the *brahma-jyoti* does not represent mature knowledge. Only by surrendering unto the Lord completely and developing one's sense of spiritual service does one reach the highest perfectional stage.

In this *mantra* the living entity prays to enter the spiritual kingdom of God after relinquishing his material body and material air. The devotee prays to the Lord to remember his activities and the sacrifices he has performed before his material body is turned into ashes. He makes this prayer at the time of death, with full consciousness of his past deeds and of the ultimate goal. One who is completely under the rule of material nature remembers the heinous activities he performed during the existence of his material body, and consequently he gets another material body after death. The *Bhagavad-gītā* (8.6) confirms this truth:

yaṁ yaṁ vāpi smaran bhāvaṁ
tyajaty ante kalevaram
taṁ tam evaiti kaunteya
sadā tad-bhāva-bhāvitaḥ

"Whatever state of being one remembers when he quits his body, O son of Kuntī, that state he will attain without fail." Thus the mind carries the living entity's propensities into the next life.

Unlike the simple animals, who have no developed mind, the dying human being can remember the activities of his life like dreams at night; therefore his mind remains surcharged with material desires, and consequently he cannot enter into the spiritual kingdom with a spiritual body. The devotees, however, develop a sense of love for Godhead by practicing devotional service to the Lord. Even if at the time of death a devotee does not remember his service to the Lord, the Lord does not forget him. This prayer is given to remind the Lord of the devotee's sacrifices, but even if there is no such reminder, the Lord does not forget the service rendered by His pure devotee.

The Lord clearly describes His intimate relationship with His devotees in the *Bhagavad-gītā* (9.30–34): "Even if one commits the most abominable action, if he is engaged in devotional service he is to be considered saintly because he is properly situated in his determination. He quickly becomes righteous and attains lasting peace. O son of Kuntī, declare it boldly that My devotee never perishes. O son of Pṛthā, those who take shelter in Me, though they be of lower birth—women, *vaiśyas* [merchants] as well as *śūdras* [workers]—can attain the supreme destination. How much more this is so of the righteous *brāhmaṇas,* the devotees and the saintly kings. Therefore, having come to this temporary, miserable world, engage in loving service unto Me. Engage your mind always in thinking of Me, become My devotee, offer obeisances to Me and worship Me. Being completely absorbed in Me, surely you will come to Me."

Śrīla Bhaktivinoda Ṭhākura explains these verses in this way: "One should regard a devotee of Kṛṣṇa to be on the right path of the saints, even though such a devotee may seem to be *su-durācāra,* 'a person of loose character.' One should try to understand the real purport of the word *su-durācāra.* A conditioned soul has to act for double functions—namely for the maintenance of the body and again for self-realization. Social status, mental development, cleanliness, austerity, nourishment and the struggle for existence are all for the maintenance of the body. The self-realization part of one's activities is executed in one's occupation as a devotee of the Lord, and one performs actions in that connection also. One must perform these two different functions along parallel lines, because a conditioned soul cannot give up the maintenance of his body. The proportion of activities for maintenance of the body decreases, however, in proportion to the increase in devotional service. As long as the proportion of devotional service does not come to the right point, there is a chance for an occasional exhibition of worldliness. But it should be noted that such worldliness cannot continue for long because, by the grace of the Lord, such imperfections will come to an end very shortly. Therefore the path of devotional service is the only right path. If one is on the right path, even an occasional occurrence of worldliness does not hamper one in the advancement of self-realization."

The facilities of devotional service are denied the impersonalists because they are attached to the *brahma-jyoti* feature of the Lord. As suggested in the previous *mantras,* they cannot penetrate the *brahma-jyoti* because they do not believe in the Personality of Godhead. Their business is mostly word jugglery and mental speculation. Consequently the impersonalists pursue a fruitless labor, as confirmed in the Twelfth Chapter of the *Bhagavad-gītā* (12.5).

All the facilities suggested in this *mantra* can be easily obtained by constant contact with the personal feature of the Absolute Truth. Devotional service to the Lord consists essentially of nine transcendental activities: (1) hearing about the Lord, (2) glorifying the Lord, (3) remembering the Lord, (4) serving the lotus feet of the Lord, (5) worshiping the Lord,

(6) offering prayers to the Lord, (7) serving the Lord, (8) enjoying friendly association with the Lord, and (9) surrendering everything unto the Lord. These nine principles of devotional service—taken all together or one by one—help a devotee remain constantly in touch with God. In this way, at the end of life it is easy for the devotee to remember the Lord. By adopting only one of these nine principles, the following renowned devotees of the Lord were able to achieve the highest perfection: (1) By hearing of the Lord, Mahārāja Parīkṣit, the hero of *Śrīmad-Bhāgavatam,* attained the desired result. (2) Just by glorifying the Lord, Śukadeva Gosvāmī, the speaker of *Śrīmad-Bhāgavatam,* attained his perfection. (3) By praying to the Lord, Akrūra attained the desired result. (4) By remembering the Lord, Prahlāda Mahārāja attained the desired result. (5) By worshiping the Lord, Pṛthu Mahārāja attained perfection. (6) By serving the lotus feet of the Lord, the goddess of fortune, Lakṣmī, attained perfection. (7) By rendering personal service to the Lord, Hanumān attained the desired result. (8) Through his friendship with the Lord, Arjuna attained the desired result. (9) By surrendering everything he had to the Lord, Mahārāja Bali attained the desired result.

Actually, the explanation of this *mantra* and of practically all the *mantras* of the Vedic hymns is summarized in the *Vedānta-sūtra* and properly explained in *Śrīmad-Bhāgavatam. Śrīmad-Bhāgavatam* is the mature fruit of the Vedic tree of wisdom. In *Śrīmad-Bhāgavatam* this particular *mantra* is explained in the questions and answers between Mahārāja Parīkṣit and Śukadeva Gosvāmī at the very beginning of their meeting. Hearing and chanting of the science of God is the basic principle of devotional life. The complete *Bhāgavatam* was heard by Mahārāja Parīkṣit and chanted by Śukadeva Gosvāmī. Mahārāja Parīkṣit inquired from Śukadeva because Śukadeva was a greater spiritual master than any great *yogī* or transcendentalist of his time.

Mahārāja Parīkṣit's main question was: "What is the duty of every man, specifically at the time of death?" Śukadeva Gosvāmī answered:

tasmād bhārata sarvātmā
bhagavān īśvaro hariḥ
śrotavyaḥ kīrtitavyaś ca
smartavyaś cecchatābhayam

"Everyone who desires to be free from all anxieties should always hear about, glorify and remember the Personality of Godhead, who is the supreme director of everything, the extinguisher of all difficulties, and the Supersoul of all living entities." (*Bhāg.* 2.1.5)

So-called human society is generally engaged at night in sleeping and having sex and during the daytime in earning as much money as possible or else in shopping for family maintenance. People have very little time to talk about the Personality of Godhead or to inquire about Him. They have dismissed God's existence in so many ways, primarily by declaring Him to be impersonal, that is, without sense perception. But in the Vedic literature—whether the *Upaniṣads, Vedānta-sūtra, Bhagavad-gītā* or *Śrīmad-Bhāgavatam*—it is declared that the Lord is a sentient being and is supreme over all other living entities. His glorious activities are identical with Himself. One should therefore not indulge in hearing and speaking of the rubbish activities of worldly politicians and so-called big men in society but should mold his life in such a way that he can engage in godly activities without wasting a second. *Śrī Īśopaniṣad* directs us toward such godly activities.

Unless one is accustomed to devotional practice, what will he remember at the time of death, when the body is dislocated, and how can he pray to the almighty Lord to remember his sacrifices? Sacrifice means denying the interest of the senses. One has to learn this art by employing the senses in the service of the Lord during one's lifetime. One can utilize the results of such practice at the time of death.

MANTRA EIGHTEEN

अग्ने नय सुपथा राये अस्मान् विश्वानि देव वयुनानि विद्वान् ।
युयोध्यस्मज्जुहुराणमेनो भूयिष्ठां ते नमउक्तिं विधेम ॥१८॥

agne naya supathā rāye asmān
viśvāni deva vayunāni vidvān
yuyodhy asmaj juhurāṇam eno
bhūyiṣṭhāṁ te nama-uktiṁ vidhema

agne—O my Lord, as powerful as fire; *naya*—kindly lead; *supathā*—by the right path; *rāye*—for reaching You; *asmān*—us; *viśvāni*—all; *deva*—O my Lord; *vayunāni*—actions; *vidvān*—the knower; *yuyodhi*—kindly remove; *asmat*—from us; *juhurāṇam*—all hindrances on the path; *enaḥ*—all vices; *bhūyiṣṭhām*—most numerous; *te*—unto You; *namaḥ uktim*—words of obeisance; *vidhema*—I do.

TRANSLATION

O my Lord, as powerful as fire, O omnipotent one, now I offer You all obeisances, falling on the ground at Your feet. O my Lord, please lead me on the right path to reach You, and since You know all that I have done in the past, please free me from the reactions to my past sins so that there will be no hindrance to my progress.

PURPORT

By surrendering to the Lord and praying for His causeless mercy, the devotee can progress on the path of complete self-realization. The Lord is addressed as fire because He can burn anything into ashes, including the sins of the surrendered soul. As described in the previous *mantras,* the real or ultimate aspect of the Absolute is His feature as the Personality of Godhead, and His impersonal *brahma-jyoti* feature is a dazzling covering over His face. Fruitive activities, or the *karma-kāṇḍa* path of self-realization, is the lowest stage in this endeavor. As soon as such activities even slightly deviate from the regulative principles of the *Vedas,* they are transformed into *vikarma,* or acts against the interest of the actor. Such *vikarma* is enacted by the illusioned living entity simply for sense gratification, and thus such activities become hindrances on the path of self-realization.

Self-realization is possible in the human form of life, but not in other forms. There are 8,400,000 species, or forms of life, of which the human form qualified by brahminical culture presents the only chance to obtain knowledge of transcendence. Brahminical culture includes truthfulness, sense control, forbearance, simplicity, full knowledge and full faith in God. It is not that one simply becomes proud of his high parentage. Just as being born the son of a big man affords one a chance to become a big man, so being born the son of a *brāhmaṇa* gives one a chance to become a *brāhmaṇa*. But such a birthright is not everything, for one still has to attain the brahminical qualifications for himself. As soon as one becomes proud of his birth as the son of a *brāhmaṇa* and neglects to acquire the qualifications of a real *brāhmaṇa,* he at once becomes degraded and falls from the path of self-realization. Thus his life's mission as a human being is defeated.

In the *Bhagavad-gītā* (6.41–42) we are assured by the Lord that the *yoga-bhraṣṭas,* or souls fallen from the path of self-realization, are given a chance to rectify themselves by taking birth either in the families of good *brāhmaṇas* or in the families of rich merchants. Such births afford higher chances for self-realization. If these chances are misused due to illusion, one loses the good opportunity of human life afforded by the almighty Lord.

The regulative principles are such that one who follows them is promoted from the platform of fruitive activities to the platform of transcendental knowledge. After many, many lifetimes of cultivating transcendental knowledge, one becomes perfect when he surrenders unto the Lord. This is the general procedure. But one who surrenders at the very beginning, as recommended in this *mantra,* at once surpasses all preliminary stages simply by adopting the devotional attitude. As stated in the *Bhagavad-gītā* (18.66), the Lord at once takes charge of such a surrendered soul and frees him from all the reactions to his sinful acts. There are many sinful reactions involved in *karma-kāṇḍa* activities, whereas in *jñāna-kāṇḍa,* the path of philosophical development, the number of such sinful activities is smaller. But in devotional service to the Lord, the path of *bhakti,* there is practically no chance of incurring sinful reactions, because a devotee of the Lord attains all the good qualifications of the Lord Himself, what to speak of those of a *brāhmaṇa*. A devotee automatically attains the qualifications of an expert *brāhmaṇa* authorized to perform sacrifices, even though the devotee may not have taken his birth in a *brāhmaṇa* family. Such is the omnipotence of the Lord. He can make a man born in a *brāhmaṇa* family as degraded as a lowborn dog-eater, and He can also make a lowborn dog-eater superior to a qualified *brāhmaṇa* simply on the strength of devotional service.

Since the omnipotent Lord is situated within the heart of everyone, He can give directions to His sincere devotees by which they can attain the right path. Such directions are especially offered to the devotee, even if he desires something else. As far as others are concerned, God gives sanction to the doer only at the risk of the doer. But in the case of a devotee, the Lord directs him in such a way that he never acts wrongly. The *Śrīmad-Bhāgavatam* (11.5.42) says:

sva-pāda-mūlaṁ bhajataḥ priyasya
tyaktānya-bhāvasya hariḥ pareśaḥ
vikarma yac cotpatitaṁ kathañcid
dhunoti sarvaṁ hṛdi sanniviṣṭaḥ

"The Lord is so kind to the devotee who is fully surrendered to His lotus feet that even though the devotee sometimes falls into the entanglement of *vikarma*—acts against the Vedic directions—the Lord at once rectifies such mistakes from within his heart. This is because the devotees are very dear to the Lord."

In this *mantra* of *Śrī Īśopaniṣad,* the devotee prays to the Lord to rectify him from within his heart. To err is human. A conditioned soul is very often apt to commit mistakes, and the only remedial measure to take against such unintentional sins is to give oneself up to the lotus feet of the Lord so that He may guide one to avoid such pitfalls. The Lord takes charge of fully surrendered souls; thus all problems are solved simply by surrendering oneself unto the Lord and acting in terms of His directions. Such directions are given to the sincere devotee in two ways: one is by way of the saints, scriptures and spiritual master, and the other is by way of the Lord Himself, who resides within the heart of everyone. Thus the devotee, fully enlightened with Vedic knowledge, is protected in all respects.

Vedic knowledge is transcendental and cannot be understood by mundane educational procedures. One can understand the Vedic *mantras* only by the grace of the Lord and the spiritual master (*yasya deve parā bhaktir yathā deve tathā gurau*). If one takes shelter of a bona fide spiritual master, it is to be understood that he has obtained the grace of the Lord. The Lord appears as the spiritual master for the devotee. Thus the spiritual master, the Vedic injunctions and the Lord Himself from within—all guide the devotee in full strength. In this way there is no chance for a devotee to fall again into the mire of material illusion. The devotee, thus protected all around, is sure to reach the ultimate destination of perfection. The entire process is hinted at in this *mantra,* and *Śrīmad-Bhāgavatam* (1.2.17–20) explains it further:

Hearing and chanting the glories of the Lord is itself an act of piety. The Lord wants everyone to hear and chant His glories because He is the well-wisher of all living entities. By hearing and chanting the glories of the Lord, one becomes cleansed of all undesirable things, and then one's devotion becomes fixed upon the Lord. At this stage the devotee acquires the brahminical qualifications, and the effects of the lower modes of nature (passion and ignorance) completely vanish. The devotee becomes fully enlightened by virtue of his devotional service, and thus he comes to know the path of the Lord and the way to attain Him. As all doubts diminish, he becomes a pure devotee.

Thus end the Bhaktivedanta Purports to Śrī Īśopaniṣad, *the knowledge that brings one nearer to the Supreme Personality of Godhead, Kṛṣṇa.*

APPENDIXES

THE AUTHOR

His Divine Grace A. C. Bhaktivedanta Swami Prabhupāda appeared in this world in 1896 in Calcutta, India. He first met his spiritual master, Śrīla Bhaktisiddhānta Sarasvatī Gosvāmī, in Calcutta in 1922. Bhaktisiddhānta Sarasvatī, a prominent religious scholar and the founder of sixty-four Gauḍīya Maṭhas (Vedic institutes), liked this educated young man and convinced him to dedicate his life to teaching Vedic knowledge. Śrīla Prabhupāda became his student and, in 1933, his formally initiated disciple.

At their first meeting, in 1922, Śrīla Bhaktisiddhānta Sarasvatī requested Śrīla Prabhupāda to broadcast Vedic knowledge in English. In the years that followed, Śrīla Prabhupāda wrote a commentary on the *Bhagavad-gītā,* assisted the Gauḍīya Maṭha in its work, and, in 1944, started *Back to Godhead,* an English fortnightly magazine. Single-handedly, Śrīla Prabhupāda edited it, typed the manuscripts, checked the galley proofs, and even distributed the individual copies. The magazine is now being continued by his followers.

In 1950 Śrīla Prabhupāda retired from married life, adopting the *vānaprastha* (retired) order to devote more time to his studies and writing. He traveled to the holy city of Vṛndāvana, where he lived in humble circumstances in the historic temple of Rādhā-Dāmodara. There he engaged for several years in deep study and writing. He accepted the renounced order of life (*sannyāsa*) in 1959. At Rādhā-Dāmodara, Śrīla Prabhupāda began work on his life's masterpiece: a multivolume commentated translation of the eighteen-thousand-verse *Śrīmad-Bhāgavatam* (*Bhāgavata Purāṇa*). He also wrote *Easy Journey to Other Planets.*

After publishing three volumes of the *Śrīmad-Bhāgavatam,* Śrīla Prabhupāda came to the United States, in September 1965, to fulfill the mission of his spiritual master. Subsequently, His Divine Grace wrote more than fifty volumes of authoritative commentated translations and summary studies of the philosophical and religious classics of India.

When he first arrived by freighter in New York City, Śrīla Prabhupāda was practically penniless. Only after almost a year of great difficulty did he establish the International Society for Krishna Consciousness, in July of 1966. Before he passed away on November 14, 1977, he had guided the Society and seen it grow to a worldwide confederation of more than one hundred *āśramas,* schools, temples, institutes, and farm communities.

In 1972 His Divine Grace introduced the Vedic system of primary and secondary education in the West by founding the *gurukula* school in Dallas, Texas. Since then his disciples have established similar schools throughout the United States and the rest of the world.

Śrīla Prabhupāda also inspired the construction of several large international cultural centers in

India. The center at Śrīdhāma Māyāpur is the site for a planned spiritual city, with the magnificent Temple of the Vedic Planetarium at its heart. In Vṛndāvana are the Kṛṣṇa-Balarāma Temple and International Guesthouse, *gurukula* school, and Śrīla Prabhupāda Memorial and Museum. There are also major cultural and educational centers in Mumbai, New Delhi, Baroda, Ahmedabad, Siliguri, Ujjain, and Ahmedabad. Other centers are either underway or planned in a dozen important locations on the Indiansubcontinent.

Śrīla Prabhupāda's most significant contribution, however, is his books. Highly respected by scholars for their authority, depth, and clarity, they are used as textbooks in numerous college courses. His writings have been translated into over fifty languages. The Bhaktivedanta Book Trust, established in 1972 to publish the works of His Divine Grace, has thus become the world's largest publisher of books in the field of Indian religion and philosophy.

In just twelve years, despite his advanced age, Śrīla Prabhupāda circled the globe fourteen times on lecture tours that took him to six continents. In spite of such a vigorous schedule, Śrīla Prabhupāda continued to write prolifically. His writings constitute a veritable library of Vedic philosophy, religion, literature, and culture.

REFERENCES

The purports of *Śrī Īśopaniṣad* are all confirmed by standard Vedic authorities. The following authentic scriptures are cited in this volume. For specific page references, consult the general index.

Atharva-veda
Bhagavad-gītā
Bhakti-rasāmṛta-sindhu
Brahma-saṁhitā
Gopāla-tāpanī Upaniṣad
Hari-bhakti-sudhodaya
Īśopaniṣad
Kaṭha Upaniṣad
Mahābhārata
Mahā Upaniṣad
Mokṣa dharma
Māṇḍūkya Upaniṣad
Nārāyaṇa Upaniṣad
Ṛg Veda
Śrīmad-Bhāgavatam
Varāha Upaniṣad
Vedānta-sūtra
Viṣṇu Purāṇa

GLOSSARY

A

Ācārya—a spiritual master; one who teaches by example.

Adhīra—one who is disturbed by material illusion.

Akarma—action that frees one from the cycle of birth and death.

Amara—deathless.

Ānanda—the Supreme Lord's aspect of bliss.

Ananta—unlimited.

Anumāna—inductive reasoning.

Apāpa-viddha—pure and uncontaminated.

Aparā prakṛti—the inferior energy of the Lord.

Apauruṣeya—not delivered by any mundane person.

Arcā-vigraha—the form of God manifested through material elements, as in a painting or statue of Kṛṣṇa worshiped in a temple or home. In this form the Lord personally accepts worship from His devotees.

Āroha—the ascending process of knowledge.

Asura—a demon.

Ātmā—the self (the body, the mind, the intellect, the Supersoul or the individual soul).

Ātma-hā—the killer of the soul.

Avidyā—ignorance.

Avyakta—the unmanifested stage of creation.

B

Bhagavān—the Supreme Personality of Godhead, possessor of all opulences in full.

Bhaktas—devotees of Śrī Kṛṣṇa.

Brahma-jyoti—the effulgence emanating from the body of the Supreme Lord and illuminating the spiritual world.

Brāhmaṇa—a person wise in Vedic knowledge, fixed in goodness, and knowledgeable of Brahman, the Absolute Truth; a member of the first Vedic social order.

Buddha—learned.

C

Cit—the Supreme Lord's aspect of knowledge.

D

Dhīra—one who is not disturbed by material illusion.

Dvija-bandhu—one born in a *brāhmaṇa* family but not qualified as a *brāhmaṇa.*

G

Guru—a spiritual master

I

Īśāvāsya—the god-centered conception.

J

Jīva-śakti—the living force.

Jñāna—knowledge; the culture of knowledge.

K

Kaniṣṭha-adhikārī—a person in the lowest stage of God realization.

Karma—material, fruitive activity and its reactions; also, fruitive actions performed in accordance with Vedic injunctions.

Karma-bandhana—work that binds one to the material world.

Karma-yoga—offering the fruit of one's work to Kṛṣṇa.

Karmīs—those engaged in activities of sense gratification.

Kṣatriya(s)—a warrior or administrator; the second Vedic social order.

M

Madhyama-adhikārīs—those in the intermediate stage of God realization.

Mahā-bhāgavata—a great personality who sees everything in relation to the Supreme Lord.

Māyā—illusion; accepting something that is not.

Māyayāpahṛta-jñānas—those whose knowledge has been stolen by illusion.

Mṛtyuloka—the place of death, the material world.

Mūḍhas—fools or asses.

N

Naiṣkarmya—*See: Akarma*
Narādhama—the lowest of human beings.
Nirguṇa—without material qualities.

P

Param brahma—the supreme spirit, i.e., the Supreme Lord, Kṛṣṇa.
Paramparā—the line of disciplic succession.
Parā prakṛti—the superior energy of the Lord.
Parā śakti—*See: Parā prakṛti*
Pitās—forefathers.
Prāṇa-vāyu—the subtle airs in the body; also, the movements of these airs.
Prasādam—food spiritualized by being offered to Kṛṣṇa.
Pratyakṣa—direct evidence.

S

Sac-cid-ānanda-vigraha—an eternal form full of knowledge and bliss.
Saguṇa—with qualities.
Sat—the Supreme Lord's aspect of eternity.
Śrīmat—a *vaiśya;* a member of the mercantile community.
Śruti—knowledge via hearing; also, the original Vedic scriptures (the *Vedas* and *Upaniṣads*), given directly by the Supreme Lord.
Śuci—a spiritually advanced *brāhmaṇa.*
Śuddha—antiseptic.
Śūdras—the worker class in society.

Śukra—omnipotent.

Sura—a godly person.

T

Tri-pād-vibhūti—the spiritual nature, which is three fourths of the Lord's energy.

U

Uttama-adhikārī—a person in the highest stage of God realization.

V

Vaikuṇṭhalokas—the planets in the spiritual sky.

Vaiśya—a famer or merchant; the third Vedic social order

Varṇāśrama—the Vedic social system of four social and four spiritual orders.

Veda—knowledge.

Vedas—the original revealed scriptures, first spoken by the Lord Himself.

Veda-vāda-ratas—those who give their own explanations of the *Vedas*.

Vidyā—knowledge.

Vikarma—sinful work, performed against scriptural injunctions.

Viṣṇu-tattva—a plenary portion of the Supreme Lord.

Y

Yoga-bhraṣṭa—a soul fallen from the path of self-realization.

SANSKRIT PRONUNCIATION GUIDE

Throughout the centuries, the Sanskrit language has been written in a variety of alphabets. The mode of writing most widely used throughout India, however, is called *devanāgarī*, which means, literally, the writing used in "the cities of the demigods." The *devanāgarī* alphabet consists of forty-eight characters: thirteen vowels and thirty-five consonants. Ancient Sanskrit grammarians arranged this alphabet according to practical linguistic principles, and this order has been accepted by all Western scholars. The system of transliteration used in this book conforms to a system that scholars have accepted to indicate the pronunciation of each Sanskrit sound.

Vowels

अ **a** आ **ā** इ **i** ई **ī** उ **u** ऊ **ū** ऋ **ṛ**

ॠ **ṝ** ऌ **ḷ** ए **e** ऐ **ai** ओ **o** औ **au**

Consonants

Gutturals:	क **ka**	ख **kha**	ग **ga**	घ **gha**	ङ **ṅa**
Palatals:	च **ca**	छ **cha**	ज **ja**	झ **jha**	ञ **ña**
Cerebrals:	ट **ṭa**	ठ **ṭha**	ड **ḍa**	ढ **ḍha**	ण **ṇa**
Dentals:	त **ta**	थ **tha**	द **da**	ध **dha**	न **na**
Labials:	प **pa**	फ **pha**	ब **ba**	भ **bha**	म **ma**
Semivowels:	य **ya**	र **ra**	ल **la**	व **va**	
Sibilants:	श **śa**	ष **ṣa**	स **sa**		
Aspirate:	ह **ha**	Anusvāra: ं **ṁ**		Visarga: ः **ḥ**	

Numerals

० – 0 १ – 1 २ – 2 ३ – 3 ४ – 4 ५ – 5 ६ – 6 ७ – 7 ८ – 8 ९ – 9

The vowels appear as follows in conjunction with a consonant:

ा **ā** ि **i** ी **ī** ु **u** ू **ū** ृ **ṛ** ॄ **ṝ** े **e** ै **ai** ो **o** ौ **au**

For example: क **ka** का **kā** कि **ki** की **kī** कु **ku** कू **kū**
कृ **kṛ** कॄ **kṝ** क्लृ **kḷ** के **ke** कै **kai** को **ko**
कौ **kau**

Generally two or more consonants in conjunction are written together in a special form, as for example: क्ष **kṣa** त्र **tra**
The vowel "**a**" is implied after a consonant with no vowel symbol. The symbol *virāma* (्) indicates that there is no final vowel: क्

The vowels are pronounced as follows:

a — as in b**u**t
ā — as in f**a**r but held twice as long as **a**
i — as in p**i**n
ī — as in p**i**que but held twice as long is **i**
u — as in p**u**sh
ū — as in r**u**le but held twice as long as **u**
ṛ — as in **ri**m
ṝ — as in **ree**d but held twice as long as **ṛ**
ḷ — as in happi**ly**
e — as in th**ey**
ai — as in **ai**sle
o — as in g**o**
au — as in h**ow**

The consonants are pronounced as follows:

Gutturals
(pronounced from the throat)

k — as in **k**ite
kh — as in Ec**kh**art
g — as in **g**ive
gh — as in di**g-h**ard
ṅ — as in si**ng**

Palatals
(pronounced with the middle of the tongue against the palate)

c — as in **ch**air
ch — as in staun**ch-h**eart
j — as in **j**oy
jh — as in he**dgeh**og
ñ — as in ca**ny**on

Cerebrals
(pronounced with the tip of the tongue against the roof of the mouth)
ṭ — as in **t**ub
ṭh — as in ligh**t-h**eart
ḍ — as in **d**ove
ḍh — as in re**d-h**ot
ṅ — as in si**ng**

Dentals
(pronounced like the cerebrals but with the tongue against the teeth)
t — as in **t**ub
th — as in ligh**t-h**eart
d — as in **d**ove
dh — as in re**d-h**ot
n — as in **n**ut

Labials
(pronounced with the lips)
p — as in **p**ine
ph — as in u**p-h**ill (not f)
b — as in **b**ird
bh — as in ru**b-h**ard
m — as in **m**other

Semivowels
y — as in **y**es
r — as in **r**un
l — as in **l**ight
v — as in **v**ine, except when preceded in the same syllable by a consonant; then as in s**w**an

Sibilants
ś — as in the German word *sprechen*
ṣ — as in **sh**ine
s — as in **s**un

Aspirate
h — as in **h**ome

Visarga
ḥ — a final h-sound: **aḥ** is pronounced like **aha**; **iḥ** like **ihi**.

Anusvara
ṁ — a resonant nasal sound as in the French word *bo***n**

There is no strong accentuation of syllables in Sanskrit, or pausing between words in a line. There is only a flowing of short and long syllables (the long twice as long as the short). A long syllable is one whose vowel is long (**ā, ī, ū, ṝ, e, ai, o, au**) or whose short vowel is followed by more than one consonant. The letters **ḥ** and **ṁ** count as consonants. Aspirated consonants (consonants followed by an **h**) count as single consonants.

INDEX OF MANTRAS

This index constitutes a complete listing of the first and third lines of each of the *mantras* of *Śrī Īśopaniṣad,* arranged in English alphabetical order. In the first column the Sanskrit transliteration is given, and in the second and third columns, respectively, the *mantra* number and page number for each verse are to be found.

INDEX OF VERSES QUOTED

This index lists the verses quoted in the purports of *Śrī Īśopaniṣad.* Numerals in boldface type refer to the first or third lines of verses quoted in full; numerals in roman type refer to partially quoted verses.

GENERAL INDEX

Numerals in boldface type indicate references to translations of the verses of *Śrī Īśopaniṣad.*

The International Society for Krishna Consciousness

Founder-*Ācārya:* His Divine Grace A.C. Bhaktivedanta Swami Prabhupāda

CENTERS AROUND THE WORLD

NORTH AMERICA

CANADA

Brampton-Mississauga, Ontario – 6 George Street South, 2nd Floor, L6Y 1P3/ Tel. (416) 648-3312/ iskconbrampton@gmail.com

Calgary, Alberta – 313 Fourth St. N.E., T2E 3S3/ Tel. (403) 265-3302/ vamanstones@shaw.ca

Edmonton, Alberta – 9353 35th Ave. NW, T6E 5R5/ Tel. (780) 439-9999/ harekrishna.edmonton@gmail.com

Montreal, Quebec – 1626 Pie IX Blvd., H1V 2C5/ Tel. (514) 521-1301/ iskconmontreal@gmail.com

◆ **Ottawa, Ontario** – 212 Somerset St. E., K1N 6V4/ Tel. (613) 565-6544/ iskconottawa@sympatico.ca

Regina, Saskatchewan – 1279 Retallack St., S4T 2H8/ Tel. (306) 525-0002 or -6461/ jagadishadas@yahoo.com

Scarborough, Ontario – 3500 McNicoll Avenue, Unit #3, M1V4C7/ Tel. (416) 300 7101/ iskconscarborough@hotmail.com

Toronto, Ontario – 243 Avenue Rd., M5R 2J6/ Tel. (416) 922-5415/ toronto@iskcon.net

Vancouver, B.C. – 5462 S.E. Marine Dr., Burnaby V5J 3G8/ Tel. (604) 433-9728/ ISKCONVancouver@gmail.com

RURAL COMMUNITY

Ashcroft, B.C. – Saranagati Dhama (mail: P.O. Box 99, V0K 1A0)/ Tel. (250) 457-7438/ Fax: (250) 453-9306/ iskconsaranagati@hotmail.com

U.S.A.

◆ **Atlanta, Georgia** – 1287 South Ponce de Leon Ave. N.E., 30306/ Tel. (404) 377-8680/ admin@atlantaharekrishnas.com

Austin, Texas – 10700 Jonwood Way, 78753/ Tel. (512) 835-2121/ sda@backtohome.com

Baltimore, Maryland –200 Bloomsbury Ave., Catonsville, 21228/ Tel. (410) 744-1624/ contact@iskconbaltimore.org

Berkeley, California – 2334 Stuart St., 94705/ Tel. (510) 540-9215/ info@iskconberkeley.net

Boise, Idaho – 1615 Martha St., 83706/ Tel. (208) 344-4274/ boise_temple@yahoo.com

Boston, Massachusetts – 72 Commonwealth Ave., 02116/ Tel. (617) 247-8611/ info@iskconboston.org

Chicago, Illinois – 1716 W. Lunt Ave., 60626/ Tel. (773) 973-0900/ chicagoiskcon@yahoo.com

Columbus, Ohio – 379 W. Eighth Ave., 43201/ Tel. (614) 421-1661/ premvilasdas.rns@gmail.com

◆ **Dallas, Texas** – 5430 Gurley Ave., 75223/ Tel. (214) 827-6330/ info@radhakalachandji.com

◆ **Denver, Colorado** – 1400 Cherry St., 80220/ Tel. (303) 333-5461/ info@krishnadenver.com

Detroit, Michigan – 383 Lenox Ave., 48215/ Tel. (313) 824-6000/ gaurangi108@hotmail.com

Gainesville, Florida – 214 N.W. 14th St., 32603/ Tel. (352) 336-4183/ kalakantha.acbsp@pamho.net

Hartford, Connecticut – 1683 Main St., E. Hartford 06108/ Tel. (860) 289-7252/ pyari108@gmail.com

Hillsboro, Oregon – 612 North 1st Ave., Hillsboro, 97124/ Tel: (503) 567-7363/ info@iskconportland.com

◆ **Honolulu, Hawaii** – Honolulu, Hawaii – 51 Coelho Way, 96817/ Tel. (808) 595-4913/ hawaii.iskcon@gmail.com

Houston, Texas – 1320 W. 34th St., 77018/ Tel. (713) 686-4482/ management@iskconhouston.org

Kansas City, Missouri – 5201 Paseo Blvd., 64110/ Tel. (816) 924-5619/ rvc@rvc.edu

Laguna Beach, California – 285 Legion St., 92651/ Tel. (949) 494-7029/ info@lagunatemple.com

◆ **Los Angeles, California** – 3764 Watseka Ave., 90034/ Tel. (310) 836-2676/ membership@harekrishnala.com

Mountain View, California – 1965 Latham St., 94040/ Tel. (650) 336-7993/ isvconnect@gmail.com

◆ **Miami, Florida** – 3220 Virginia St., 33133 (mail: 3109 Grand Ave. #491, Coconut Grove, FL 33133)/ Tel. (305) 461-1348/ devotionalservice@iskcon-miami.org

New Orleans, Louisiana – 2936 Esplanade Ave., 70119/ Tel. (504) 304-0032 (office) or (504)

To save space, we've skipped the codes for North America (1) and India (91).

◆ Temples with restaurants or dining

638-1944 (temple) / gopal211@aol.com
◆ **New York, New York** – 305 Schermerhorn St., Brooklyn 11217/ Tel. (718) 855-6714/ ramabhadra@aol.com
Orlando, Florida – 2651 Rouse Rd., 32817/ Tel. (407) 257-3865/ info@iskconorlando.com
Philadelphia, Pennsylvania – 41 West Allens Lane, 19119/ Tel. (215) 247-4600/ Fax: (215) 247-8702/ savecows@aol.com
◆ **Philadelphia, Pennsylvania** – 1408 South St., 19146/ Tel. (215) 985-9303/ info@iskconphiladelphia.com
Phoenix, Arizona – 100 S. Weber Dr., Chandler, 85226/ Tel. (480) 705-4900/ premadhatridd@gmail.com
Plainfield, New Jersey– 1020 W. 7th St., 07063/ Tel. (973) 519-3374/ harekrsna@iskconnj.com
◆ **St. Louis, Missouri** – 3926 Lindell Blvd., 63108/ Tel. (314) 535-8085 or 534-1708/ rpsdas@gmail.com
Salt Lake City, Utah – 965 E. 3370 South, 84106/ Tel. (801) 487-4005/ utahkrishnas@gmail.com
San Antonio, Texas – 6772 Oxford Trace, 78240/ Tel. (210) 420-1182/ aadasa@gmail.com
◆ **San Diego, California** – 1030 Grand Ave., Pacific Beach 92109/ Tel. (858) 429-9375/ krishna.sandiego@gmail.com
Seattle, Washington – 1420 228th Ave. S.E., Sammamish 98075/ Tel. (425) 246-8436/ info@vedicculturalcenter.org
◆ **Spanish Fork, Utah** – Krishna Temple Project & KHQN Radio, 8628 S. State Rd., 84660/ Tel. (801) 798-3559/ carudas@earthlink.net
Tallahassee, Florida – 4601 Crawfordville Rd., 32305/ Tel. 850-727-5785/ tallahassee.iskcon@gmail.com
Towaco, New Jersey – 100 Jacksonville Rd., 07082/ Tel. (973) 299-0970/ madhupati.jas@pamho.net
◆ **Tucson, Arizona** – 711 E. Blacklidge Dr., 85719/ Tel. (520) 792-0630/ sandaminidd@cs.com
Washington, D.C. – 10310 Oaklyn Dr., Potomac, Maryland 20854/ Tel. (301) 299-2100/ info@iskconofdc.org

RURAL COMMUNITIES

◆ **Alachua, Florida** (New Raman Reti) – 17306 N.W. 112th Blvd., 32615 (mail: P.O. Box 819, 32616)/ Tel. (386) 462-2017/ Fax: (386) 462-2641/ alachuatemple@gmail.com
Carriere, Mississippi (New Talavan) – 31492 Anner Road, 39426/ Tel. (601) 213-3586/ newtalavan@gmail.com
Gurabo, Puerto Rico (New Govardhana Hill) – Carr. 181, Km. 16.3, Bo. Santa Rita, Gurabo (mail: HC-01, Box 8440, Gurabo, PR 00778)/ Tel. (787) 367-3530 or (787) 737-1722/ manonatha@gmail.com
Hillsborough, North Carolina (New Goloka) – 1032 Dimmocks Mill Rd., 27278/ Tel. (919) 732-6492/ bkgoswami@earthlink.net
◆ **Moundsville, West Virginia (New Vrindaban)** – R.D. No. 1, Box 319, Hare Krishna Ridge, 26041/ Tel. (304) 843-1600; Guesthouse, (304) 845-5905/ mail@newvrindaban.com
Mulberry, Tennessee (Murari-sevaka) – 532 Murari Lane, 37359/ Tel. (931) 759-6888/ murari_sevaka@yahoo.com
Port Royal, Pennsylvania (Gita Nagari) – 534 Gita Nagari Rd./ Tel. (717) 527-4101/ dhruva.bts@pamho.net
Sandy Ridge, North Carolina – Prabhupada Village, 1283 Prabhupada Rd., 27046/ Tel. (336) 593-2322/ madanmohanmohini72@gmail.com

ADDITIONAL RESTAURANTS

Hato Rey, Puerto Rico – Tamal Krishna's Veggie Garden, 131 Eleanor Roosevelt, 00918/ Tel. (787) 754-6959/ tkveggiegarden@aol.com

ASIA

INDIA

Agartala, Tripura – Matchow Muhani, Assam-Agatala Rd., Banamalipur 799 001/ Tel. (381) 2327053 or 9436167045/ premadatadas@rediffmail.com
Ahmedabad, Gujarat – Satellite Rd., Gandhinagar Highway, Bopal Crossing, 380 059/Tel. (79) 2686-1945, -1644, or -2350/ jasomatinandan.acbsp@pamho.net
Allahabad, UP – Hare Krishna Dham, 161 Kashi Raj Nagar, Baluaghat 211 003/Tel. (532) 2416718/ iskcon.allahabad@pamho.net
Amravati, Maharashtra – Saraswati Colony, Rathi Nagar 444 603/ Tel. (721) 2666849 or 9421805105/ iskconamravati@ymail.com
Amritsar, Punjab – Chowk Moni Bazar, Laxmansar, 143 001/ Tel. (183) 2540177
Aravade, Maharashtra – Hare Krishna Gram, Tal. Tasgaon, Dist. Sangli/ Tel. (2346) 255766 or 255515, or 09371163955/ iskcon.aravade@pamho.net
Bangalore, Karnataka – ISKCON Sri Jagannath Mandir, No. 5 Sripuram, 1st cross, Sheshadripuram, Bangalore 560 020/ Tel. 9901060738 or 9886709603/ varada.krsna.jps@pamho.net

Baroda, Gujarat – Hare Krishna Land, Gotri Rd., 390 021/ Tel. (265) 2310630 or 2331012/ iskcon.baroda@pamho.net
Beed, Maharashtra – Saint Sawata Mali Chowk, MIDC Road, Beed 431 122/ Tel. (2442) 231799 or 233054
Belgaum, Karnataka – 211 Shukravar Peth, Tilak Wadi, 590 006/ Tel. (831) 2436267, or 2400108, or 4204672/ iskcon.belgaum@pamho.net
Bhadrak, Odisha – Gour Gopal Mandir, Kuansh Bhadrak 756 100/ Tel. (6784) 251730
◆ **Bhubaneswar, Odisha** – N.H. No. 5, IRC Village, 751 015/ Tel. (674) 2553517, 2553475, or 2554283/ gm.iskconbbsr.ggs@pamho.net
Brahmapur, Odisha – Hare Krishna Temple, N. H. No. 5, Dist. Ganjam, 760 008/ Tel. (680) 2116100 or 9437179400/ pancharatna.gkg@pamho.net
Brahmapur, Odisha – Sri Ram Govinda Mandir, Aska Rd., at Post Ankuspur, Brahmapur, Dist. Ganjam, 761 100/ Tel. (680) 2485720/ srigopalccd@yahoo.co.in
Chamorshi, Maharashtra – 78, Krishna Nagar, Chamorshi 264 403, Dist. Gadchiroli, Chamorshi 264 403/ Tel. 09423422914
Chandigarh, Punjab – Hare Krishna Dham, Sector 36-B, 160 036/ Tel. (172) 260-1590 or 260-3232/ iskcon.chandigarh@pamho.net
Chennai, TN – Hare Krishna Land, off ECR, Akkarai, Sholinganallur, Chennai 600 119/ Tel. (44) 24530921 or 24530923/ iskconchennai@gmail.com
Coimbatore, TN – Jagannath Mandir, Hare Krishna Land, Aerodrome P.O., Opp. CIT, 641 014/ Tel. (422) 257-4508, 257-4812, or 257-4813/ info@iskcon-coimbatore.org
Dwarka, Gujarat – Bharatiya Bhavan, Devi Bhavan Rd., 361 335/ Tel. (2892) 34606
Gadei Giri, Odisha – Post Alabol Via Balikuda, Dist. Jagatsinghpur, 754 108/ (6724) 238112/ srigopalccd@yahoo.co.in
Ghaziabad, UP – Hare Krishna Marg, R-11/35, Raj Nagar, 201 002/ Tel. 9312438001 or 9312438000/ iskcon.ghaziabad@pamho.net
Guntur, AP – Opp. Sivalayam, Peda Kakani 522 509
Guwahati, Assam – Ulubari Chariali, South Sarania, 781 007/ Tel. (361) 2525963/ iskcon.guwahati@pamho.net
Hanumkonda, AP – Neeladri Rd., Kapuwada, 506 011/ Tel. (8712) 77399
Haridaspur, WB – P.O. Chhaygharia, Bangaon, 24 Parganas 743 704/ Tel. (3215) 57856
Haridwar, Uttaranchal – Prabhupada Ashram, G. House, Nai Basti, Mahadev Nagar, Bhimgoda, 249 401/ Tel. (1334) 260818 or 9411371870
Hyderabad, AP – Hare Krishna Land, Nampally Station Rd., 500 001/ Tel. 8106130279 or (40) 24744969/ iskcon.hyderabad@pamho.net; Guesthouse: guesthouse.iskconhyd@pamho.net
Imphal, Manipur – Hare Krishna Land, Airport Rd., 795 001/ Tel. (385) 2455693/ manimandir@sancharnet.in
Indore, MP – ISKCON, Nipania, Indore/ Tel. 9300474043/ mahaman.acbsp@pamho.net
Jaipur, Rajasthan – Sri Sri Giridhari Dauji Mandir, ISKCON Rd., Village Dholai (Opp. Vijay Path), Mansarovar, New Sanganer Rd., Jaipur 302020 (mail: ISKCON, 117/326 Agarwal Farm, Mansarovar, Jaipur 302 020)/ Tel. (141) 2782765, 2781860, or (mobile) 9351549864/ jaipur@pamho.net
Jhansi, UP – Inside Saiyar Gate, Near Kali Badi/ Tel. (510) 2443602
Kanpur, UP – Mainawati Marg, Bithur Rd., Nawabganj, 208 002/ Tel. 9037188117, 9198707801, or 9198707804/ iskcon.kanpur@pamho.net
Katra, J&K – Srila Prabhupada Ashram, Sri Kalika Mata Mandir, Katra Vaishnodevi, 182 101/ Tel. (1991) 233047
Kolkata, WB – 3C Albert Rd. 700 017 (behind Minto Park, opp. Birla High School), / Tel. (33) 3028-9258 or -9280/ iskcon.calcutta@pamho.net
◆ **Kurukshetra, Haryana** – ISKCON, Main Bazaar, 136 118/ Tel. (1744) 234806 or 235529
Lucknow, UP – 1 Ashok Nagar, Guru Govind Singh Marg, 226 018/ Tel. (522) 2636500, 9415235050, or 9415008065/ lucknow@pamho.net
Ludhiana, Punjab – Sterling Tower, Vrindavan Rd., Civil Lines, 141001/ Tel. 9316970600 or (161) 2770600, / iskcon.ludhiana@pamho.net
Madurai, TN – 37 Maninagaram Main Road, 625 001/ Tel. (452) 274-6472
Mangalore, Karnataka – ISKCON Sri Jagannath Mandir, near Hotel Woodlands, Bunts Hostel Rd., 575 003/ Tel. (824) 2423326, 2442756, or 9844325616
◆ **Mayapur, WB** – ISKCON, Shree Mayapur Chandrodaya Mandir, Shree Mayapur Dham, Dist. Nadia, 741 313/ Tel. (3472) 245620, 245240, or 245355/ mayapur.chandrodaya@pamho.net
Moirang, Manipur – Nongban Enkhol, Tidim Rd./ Tel. (3879) 795133

◆ **Mumbai (Bombay), Maharashtra** – Hare Krishna Land, Juhu 400 049/ Tel. (22) 26206860/ info@iskconmumbai.com; guest.house.bombay@pamho.net
◆ **Mumbai, Maharashtra** – 7 K. M. Munshi Marg, Chowpatty 400 007/ Tel. (22) 23665500/ info@radhagopinath.com
Mumbai, Maharashtra – Shristhi Complex, Mira Rd. (E), opposite Royal College, Dist. Thane, 401 107/ Tel. (22) 2811-7795 or -7796/ jagjivan.gkg@pamho.net
Mysore, Karnataka – #31, 18th Cross, Jayanagar, 570 014/ Tel. (821) 2500582 or 6567333/ mysore.iskcon@gmail.com
Nagpur, Maharashtra – Empress City Mall, Opp. Raman Science Centre, Gandhi Sagar Lake, 440017/ Tel. 9049828549, 9823014688, or 9766447719/ iskcon.nagpur@pamho.net
Nellore, AP – ISKCON City, Hare Krishna Rd., 524 004/ Tel. (861) 2314577 or 9215536589/ sukadevaswami@gmail.com
◆ **New Delhi, UP** – Hare Krishna Hill, Sant Nagar Main Rd., East of Kailash, 110 065/ Tel. (011) 2623-5133, 4, 5, 6, or 7/ delhi@pamho.net; (Guesthouse: guest.house.new.delhi@pamho.net)
New Delhi, UP – 41/77, Punjabi Bagh (West), 110 026/ Tel. (11) 25222851 or 25227478/ iskcon.punjabi.bagh@pamho.net
Noida, UP – A-5, Sector-33, 201 301 (Opposite NTPC office)/ Tel. (120) 2506211
Pandharpur, Maharashtra – Hare Krishna Dhama, East Bank of Chandrabhaga River, Pandharpur, Dist. Solapur, 413 304/ Tel. (2186) 267242, 267266, or 9423335991/ iskcon.pandharpur@pamho.net
Patna, Bihar – Sri Sri Banke Bihariji Mandir, Golok Dham, Budha Marg, Patna-1/ Tel. (612) 2220794, 2687637, 2685081, or 9431021881/ krishna.kripa.jps@pamho.net
Pondicherry – No. 2b, First floor, 7th Crosscutting (above Sai Departmental Stores), Krishna Nagar Main Road, Krishna Nagar, Lawspet, Pondicherry 605 008/ Tel. (0413) 2210402 or (mobile) 09940864086 or 08190018108/ iskconpondy@gmail.com
Pune, Maharashtra – 4 Tarapoor Rd., Camp, 411 001/ Tel. (20) 41033222 or 41033223/ nvcc@iskconpune.in
Puri, Odisha – Bhakti Kuti, Swargadwar, 752 001/ Tel. (6752) 231440
Raipur, Chhatisgarh – Hare Krishna Land, Alopi Nagar, Opposite Maharshi Vidyalaya, Tatibandh, Raipur 492 001/ Tel. (771) 5037555/ or 9893276985/ iskconraipur@yahoo.com
Rajkot, Gujarat – Sri Sri Radha Neelmadhav Dham, Kalawad Rd., opposite Kankot Patiya, Mota Mava, 360 005/ Tel. 9898550185/ vaishnavseva@yahoo.co.in
Ranaghat, WB – Gourdham, Habibpur, Ranaghat, Dist. Nadia, 741 403/ Tel. (3473) 281150 or 281226/ shyamrup.jps@pamho.net
Salem, TN – ISKCON, Hare Krishna Land, Karuppur 636 012/ Tel. (427) 2001686/ iskcon.salem@pamho.net
Secunderabad, AP – 27 St. John's Rd., 500 026/ Tel. (40) 780-5232
Silchar, Assam – Ambikapatti, Silchar, Dist. Cachar, 788 004/ Tel. (3842) 34615
Siliguri, WB – ISKCON Road, Gitalpara, 734 406/ Tel. (353) 426619, 539046, or 539082
Solapur, Maharashtra – Hare Krishna Land, 171/2 Uttar Kasabe, Akkalkot Rd., Bhaktivedanta Marg, Near New Jakat Naka, Dist. Solapur, 413006/ Tel. 9371178393 or 9370651251/ shursendas@yahoo.co.in
Srirangam, TN – 103 Amma Mandapam Rd., Sri Rangam, Trichy 620 006/ Tel. (431) 2433945/ iskcon_srirangam@yahoo.co.in
Surat, Gujarat – Ashram Rd., Jahangirpura, 395 005/ Tel. (261) 276-5891 or 276-5516/ surat@pamho.net
Thiruvananthapuram (Trivandrum), Kerala – Hospital Rd., Thycaud, 695 014/ Tel. (471) 2328197/ jsdasa@yahoo.co.in
Tirunelveli, TN – 10B Tiruvananthapuram, Near Vannarapettai Circle, 627 002/ Tel. (462) 2501640
◆ **Tirupati, AP** – K.T. Rd., Vinayaka Nagar, 517 507/ Tel. (877) 2231760 or 2230009/ revati.raman.jps@pamho.net (Guestouse: guesthouse.tirupati@pamho.net)
Udhampur, J&K – Srila Prabhupada Ashram, Srila Prabhupada Marg, Srila Prabhupada Nagar, 182 101/ Tel. (1992) 270298/ info@iskconudhampur.com
Ujjain, MP – 35–37 Hare Krishna Land, Bharatpuri, 456 010/ Tel. (734) 2535000, 2531000, or 9300969016/ iskcon.ujjain@pamho.net
Vallabh Vidyanagar, Gujarat – Opp. B&B Polytechnic, Mota Bazaar, Dist. Anand, 388 120/ Tel. (26192) 230796 or 233012/ iskcon.vvnagar@pamho.net
Varanasi, UP – ISKCON, B 27/80 Durgakund Rd., Near Durgakund Police Station, Varanasi 221 010/ Tel. (542) 276422 or 222617
Vellore, TN – Chennai Ext. Centre, 10–12, 10th East Cross Rd., Gandhi Nagar, 632 006

Vijayawada, AP — Venkatapalem Karakatta Rd., Undavalli Village, Tadepalli Mandaal, Vijayawada, Dist. Guntur 522 501/ Tel. (8645) 272513/ mmdasiskconvijayawada@gmail.com

Visakhapatnam, AP — Hare Krishna Land, Sagaranagar-45 (City office and mail: Plot No. 52, Pandurangapuram Beach Rd., Visakhapatnam 530 043)/ Tel. (891) 2528376 or 6537625/ samba.jps@pamho.net (Guesthouse: guesthouse.vizag@pamho.net)

♦ **Vrindavan, UP** — Krishna-Balaram Mandir, Bhaktivedanta Swami Marg, Raman Reti, Mathura Dist., 281 124/ Tel. (565) 2540728/ iskcon.vrindavan@pamho.net (Guesthouse: Tel. (565) 2540022/ ramamani@sancharnet.in

Warangal, AP — Mulugu Rd., Ayappa Pidipally, 506 007/ Tel. (8712) 426182

Yamunanagar, Haryana — ISKCON Hare Krishna Dham, Hare Krishna Marg, Raghunathpuri, Yamunanagar 135001/ Tel. (1732) 321001 or (mobile) 09355330775/ vishnu_bakshi05@yahoo.co.in

RURAL COMMUNITIES

Ahmedabad District, Gujarat (Hare Krishna Farm) — Katwada (contact ISKCON Ahmedabad)

Assam — Karnamadhu, Dist. Karimganj

Chamorshi, Maharashtra — 78 Krishnanagar Dham, Dist. Gadhachiroli, 442 603/ Tel. (218) 623473

Hyderabad, AP (New Naimisaranya Farm) — P.O. Dabilpur Village, Medchal Tq., Dist. R.R., 501 401/ Tel. (40) 65520070 or 9440057263/ naimisaranya@pamho.net

Indore, MP (Krishna-Balarama Mandir) — Hare Krishna Vihar, Nipania Village/ Tel. (731) 572794

Mayapur, WB — (contact ISKCON Mayapur)

Puri, Odisha — ISKCON, Bhaktivedanta Ashram, Sipasirubuli, 752 001/ Tel. (6752) 230494

Surat, Gujarat — Bhaktivedanta Rajavidyalaya, Krishnalok, Surat-Bardoli Rd. Gangapur, P.O. Gangadhara, Dist. Surat, 394 310/ Tel. (2622) 63546

Vrindavan, UP — Vrinda Kund, Nandagaon, Dist. Mathura, U.P.

ADDITIONAL RESTAURANT

Kolkata, WB — Govinda's, ISKCON House, 22 Gurusaday Rd., 700 019/ Tel. (33) 24756922 or 24749009

Surat, Gujarat — Ashram Rd., Jahangirpura 395005/ Tel. (261) 2765891 or 2765516

MALAYSIA

Bahau — 156 Taman Sornam, Bahau 72100, Negeri Sembilan/ Tel. +60 (6) 481-4350 or 454-8982/ paramanandakp@yahoo.com

Bukit Mertajam — 429 Jalan Sungai Rambai, 14000 Bukit Mertajam/ Tel. +60 (4) 538-1276/ arumugam@notes.asemal.com.my

Ipoh — 15-H Jalan Lang, Jalan Padang, Tembak, 30000 Ipoh Perak, Darul Ridzuan/ Tel. +60 (5) 506-1601

Klang — No. 20, Lorong Besi 4, Off Jl. Teluk Pulai, Selangor D.E., 41100/ Tel. +60 (12) 6342464, (12) 3179206 or (603) 33712060/ ramram991@yahoo.com

Kuala Lumpur — Lot 9901, Jalan Awan Jawa, Taman Yarl, 58200 Kuala Lumpur/ Tel. +60 (3) 7980-7355/ president@iskconkl.com

Kuching — Lot 680, Block 250, Lorong Ketitir 3, Batu Kawa, 93250 Kuching, Sarawak/ Tel. +60 (82) 688-708/ kripa@tm.net.my

Penang — 43A Jalan Kebun Bunga, 11350 Penang/ Tel. +60 (4) 229-5958/ isana_gauranga@hotmail.com

Prai — 3051 Lorong Jelawat 4, Seberang Jaya, 13700 Prai/ Tel. +60 43808897 or 43809989/ kaleshadas@gmail.com

Seremban—28/7J Taman Desa, Temiang, 70200 Seremban, Negeri Sembilan (mail: 14 RJ 1/1, Taman Rasah Jaya, 70300 Seremban, Negeri Sembilan)/ Tel. +60 (6) 765-1379/ ppnada@tm.net.my

Sungei Petani — Lot 46, Jalan 1/6, Taman Sri Wang, 08000 Sungei Petani/ abbay_143@hotmail.com

Taiping — 24 Lorong Panglima (Cator Ave.), Assam Kumbang, 34000 Taiping, Perak D.R. (mail: 590 Jalan Wat Siam, Kampung Pinang, 34600 Kamunting, Taiping, Perak)/ Tel. +60 (5) 807-9702 or 808-1475

Teluk Intan — Jalan Sungai Manik, 36000 Teluk Intan, Perak/ Tel. +63 (32) 83254

OTHER COUNTRIES

Alaminos, Philippines — 3rd/4th Floors, Donato's Trading Building, F. Fule Street, Alaminos, Laguna 4001/ Tel. +63 (49) 5672104 or 9106576483/ iskcon.philippines@yahoo.com

Bangkok, Thailand — Soi 3, Tanon Itsarapap, Toonburi/ Tel. +66 29445346, 814455401, or 897810623/ swami.bvv.narasimha@pamho.net

Chittagong, Bangladesh — Caitanya Cultural Society, 23 Nandan Kanan, N. N. Paul Blvd./ Tel. + 880 (31) 610822

Chittagong, Bangladesh — Sri Krishna Mandir, in front of Afmi Plaza, Prabartak Sangha (mail: P.O. Box 440)/ Tel. +880 (31) 2551950, 610822, or 1819395948/ iskconctg@gmail.com

Colombo, Sri Lanka – 188 New Chetty St., Colombo 13/ Tel. +94 (11) 2433325/ iskcon@slt.lk
Denpasar, Indonesia – Radha-Rasesvara Mandir, Jl. Tanah Putih, Gg. Tanah Ayu, Blumbungan, Sibang Gede, Abiansemal, Badung, Bali, 80352/ Tel. +62 (361) 228391, 462596, or 3145052/ iskcon_id@yahoo.com
Dhaka, Bangladesh – 5 Chandra Mohon Basak St., Banagram, 1203/ Tel. +880 (2) 236249/ iskcon_bangladesh@yahoo.com
Dhaka, Bangladesh – 79 Swamibag, Dhaka-11/ Tel. +880 (2) 7122747 or 7122488/ info@iskconbd.org
Hong Kong, China – 6/F Oceanview Court, 27 Chatham Rd. South (mail: P.O. Box 98919)/ Tel. +852 2739-6818/ iskconhk@iskconhk.org
Jakarta, Indonesia – Yayasan Radha-Govinda, P.O. Box 2694, Jakarta Pusat 10001/ Tel. +62 (21) 489-9646/ matsyads@bogor.wasantara.net.id
Jessore, Bangladesh – Nitai Gaur Mandir, Kathakhali Bazaar P.O., Panjia
Jessore, Bangladesh – Sri Rup-Sanatan Smriti Tirtha Mandir, Ramshara, Magurahat P.O., Abhaynagar
Kathmandu, Nepal – Budhanilkantha (mail: GPO Box 3520)/ Tel. +977 (1) 4373790 or 4373786/ iskconkathmandu@gmail.com
Kuala Lumpur, Malaysia – Lot 9901, Jalan Awan Jawa, Taman Yarl, 58200 Kuala Lumpur/ Tel. +60 (3) 7980-7355/ contact.iskcon@gmail.com
Mandalay, Myanmar – ISKCON Sri Krishna Temple, Corner of 19th Thukha St., Nanshe, Mandalay/ sdas108@hotmail.com
Manila, Philippines – #9105 Banuyo St., San Antonio Village, Makati City/ Tel. +63 (2) 8901947 or 8963357/ iskconmanila@yahoo.com
Myitkyina, Myanmar – ISKCON Sri Jagannath Temple, Bogyoke St., Shansu Taung, Myitkyina, Kachin State/ mahanadi@mptmail.net.mm
Osafia, Israel – P.O. Box 2232, Osafia Village 30090/ Tel. +972 (4) 839-2876
Osaka, Japan – 1-1-17 Katamachi, Miyakojima-ku, Osaka 534-0025/ Tel. +81 (6) 6352-0729
Sylhet, Bangladesh – Yugal Tila, Kajalshah, Opp. Osmani Medical College, Gate No. 1, Sylhet 03100/ Tel. +880 821721358, 1711478190, or 1718781144/ info@iskconsylhet.com
Tokyo, Japan – 2-23-4 Funabori, Edogawa-ku, Tokyo 134-0091/ Tel. +81 (3) 3877-3000/ iskcon.new.gaya.japan@gmail.com
Yogyakarta, Indonesia – P.O. Box 25, Babarsari YK, DIY

RURAL COMMUNITIES
Bangladesh (Kulaura) – Rangirkul Bidyashram, Kulaura, Dist. Moulvibazar/ Fax: +880 (8624) 88035
Bangladesh (Sri Pundarika Dhama) – Mekhla, Hathazari, Dist. Chittagong/ Tel. +880 (31) 610822
Bangladesh (Comilla) – Jagannathpur, Comilla
Indonesia (Govinda Kunja) – (contact ISKCON Jakarta)

RESTAURANTS
Tokyo – Vegetable-Kitchen Govinda's, 5-17-10 Nakano, Nakano-ku, Tokyo 164-0001/Tel. +81 (3) 3387-8998; govindas_murata@yahoo.co.jp
Tokyo – Devadeva Cafe, 2-14-7 Kichijoji-Honcho, Musashino-City, Tokyo/ Tel. +81 (422) 21-6220/ info@devadevacafe.com

EUROPE

UNITED KINGDOM AND IRELAND

Belfast, Northern Ireland – Sri Sri Radha-Madhava Mandir, Brooklands, 2A Brooklands Grange, Belfast BT17 0HE/ Tel. +44 (28) 9062 0530/ hk.temple108@gmail.com
Birmingham, England – 84 Stanmore Rd., Edgbaston B16 9TB/ Tel. +44 (121) 420 4999/ iskconbirmingham@gmail.com
Cardiff, Wales – Cafe Atma / The Soul Centre, 40 Crwys Road, Cathays, CF24 4NN/ +44 (29) 20 390 391/ cafe.atma@gmail.com
Coventry, England – Kingfield Rd., Coventry (mail: 19 Gloucester St., Coventry CV1 3BZ)/ Tel. +44 (24) 7655 2822 or -5420/ haridas.kds@pamho.net
♦ **Dublin, Ireland** – 83 Middle Abbey St., Dublin 1/ Tel. +353 (1) 661 5095/ dublin@krishna.ie; Govinda's: info@govindas.ie
Lesmahagow, Scotland – Karuna Bhavan, Bankhouse Rd., Lesmahagow, Lanarkshire, ML11 0ES/ Tel. +44 (1555) 894790/ karunabhavan@aol.com
Leicester, England – 31 Granby Street, LE1 6EP/ Tel. +44 (0) 7597 786 676/ pradyumna.jas@pamho.net
♦ **London, England (city)** – Radha-Krishna Temple, 10 Soho Street, London W1D 3DL/ Tel. +44 (20) 7437 3662; shop, 7440 5221; Govinda's Restaurant, 7440 5229/ info@iskcon-london.org
♦ **London, England (country)** – Bhaktivedanta Manor, Dharam Marg, Hilfield Lane, Watford, Herts, WD25 8EZ/ Tel. +44 (1923) 851000/ info@krishnatemple.com; Guesthouse: bmguesthouse@krishna.com
London, England (south) – 42 Enmore Road,

South Norwood, SE25 5NG/ Tel. +44 7988857530/ krishnaprema89@hotmail.com
London, England (Kings Cross) — 102 Caledonain Rd., Kings Cross, Islington, N1 9DN/ Tel. +44 (20) 7168 5732/ foodforalluk@aol.com
Manchester, England — 20 Mayfield Rd., Whalley Range, M16 8FT/ Tel. +44 (161) 226 4416/ contact@iskconmanchester.com
Newcastle-upon-Tyne, England — 304 Westgate Rd., NE4 6AR/ Tel. +44 (191) 272 1911
♦ **Swansea, Wales** — Govinda's, 8 Craddock St., SA1 3EN/ Tel. +44 (1792) 468469/ info@iskconwales.org.uk; restaurant, info@govindas.org.uk

RURAL COMMUNITIES

Upper Lough Erne, Northern Ireland — Govindadwipa Dhama, Inisrath Island, Derrylin, Co. Fermanagh, BT92 9GN/ Tel. +44 (28) 6772 3878/ govindadwipa@pamho.net
London, England — (contact Bhaktivedanta Manor) Programs are held regularly in more than forty other cities in the UK. For information, contact ISKCON Reader Services, P.O. Box 730, Watford WD25 8EZ, UK

ADDITIONAL RESTAURANTS

Dublin, Ireland — Govinda's, 4 Aungier St., Dublin 2/ Tel. +353 (1) 475 0309/ info@govindas.ie
Dublin, Ireland — Govinda's, 18 Merrion Row, Dublin 2/ Tel. +353 (1) 661 5095/ praghosa.sdg@pamho.net
Dublin, Ireland — Govinda's, 83 Middle Abbey St., Dublin 1/ Tel. +353 (1) 661 5095/ info@govindas.ie
Nottingham, England — Govinda's Nottingham, 7–9 Thurland Street, NG1 3DR/ Tel. +44 115 985 9639/ govindasnottingham@gmail.com

GERMANY

Abentheuer — Bückingstr. 4a-8, 55767 Abentheuer/ Tel. +49: (6782) 2214 or (6782) 109 845/ info@goloka-dhama.de
♦ **Cologne** — Taunusstr. 40, 51105/ Tel. +49 (221) 8303778/ keshava.bbs@gauradesh.com
Hamburg — Eiffestrasse 424, 20537/ Tel. +49 (40) 4102848/ vaidac@aol.com
Heidelberg — Forum 5, Wohnung 4, 69126/ Tel. & fax: +49 (6221) 384553/ vipula@pamho.net
Leipzig — Stöckelstrasse 60, 04347/ Tel. +49 (341) 2348055/ sadbhuja@gmx.net
Munich — Wachenheimer Strasse 1, 81539/ Tel. +49 (89) 68800288/ iskcon.muenchen@krishnatempel.de
Trier — Boecking Str. 4a, 55767 Abentheuer/ Tel. +49 (6782) 980436/ Fax: +49 (6782) 980437/ info@goloka-dhama.de
Wiesbaden — Aarstrasse 8B, 65329 Burg Hohenstein/ Tel. +49 (6120) 904107/ iskcon.wiesbaden@web.de

RURAL COMMUNITY

Passau (Simhachalam) — Zielberg 20, 94118 Jandelsbrunn/ Tel +49 (8583) 316/ info@simhachalam.de

ADDITIONAL RESTAURANT

Cologne — Govindam, Roonstrasse 3, 50674 Köln

HUNGARY

Budapest — III. Lehel Street 15–17 (Csillaghedy), 1039 Budapest/ Tel. +36 (1) 391-0435 or 397-5219/ Fax: (60) 514114/ budapest@pamho.net
Eger — Szechenyi u. 64, 3300 Eger/ Tel. +36 (36) 313-761/ eger@pamho.net
Pecs — Damjanich u. 22, 7624 Pecs/ Tel. +36 (72) 515-991/ Fax: (72) 313-771/ pecs@pamho.net

RURAL COMMUNITY

Somogyvamos — Krsna-völgy, Fö u. 38, 8699 Somogyvamos/ Tel. & fax: +36 (85) 540-002 or 340-185/ info@krisnavolgy.hu

RESTAURANT

Budapest — Govinda Restaurant, Vigyazo Ferenc St. 4, 1051 Budapest/ Tel. +36 (1) 269-1625 or 302-2284/ Fax: (01) 473-1310

ITALY

Bergamo — Villaggio Hare Krishna (da Medolago strada per Terno d'Isola), 24040 Chignolo d'Isola (BG)/ Tel. +39 (035) 4940705/ Fax: +39 (035) 199622233/ villagio.hare.krsna@hare.krsna.it
Catania — via della Regione 16 - Tarderia, 95030 Pedara CT/ Tel. +39 (095) 7896216
♦ **Rome** — Govinda Centro Hare Krsna, via Santa Maria del Pianto, 16, 00186/ Tel. +39 (06) 68891540/ govinda.roma@harekrsna.it
Vicenza — via Roma 9, 36020 Albettone (VI)/ Tel. +39 (0444) 790573/ Fax: +39 (0444) 790581/ prabhupadadesh@pamho.net

RURAL COMMUNITY

♦ **Florence** (Villa Vrindavan) — via Scopeti 108, 50026 San Casciano in Val di Pesa (FI)/ Tel. +39 (055) 820054/ Fax: +39 (055) 828470/ isvaripriya@libero.it

RESTAURANT

Milan — Govinda's, via Valpetrosa 5, 20123/ Tel. +39 (02) 862417

SPAIN

Barcelona — Plaza Reial 12, Entlo 2, 08002/ Tel.

+34 93 302-5194/ templobcn@hotmail.com
Madrid – Espíritu Santo 19, 28004/ Tel. +34 91 521-3096
Málaga – Ctra. Alora, 3, Int., 29140 Churriana/ Tel. +34 95 262-1038/ info@harekrishnamalaga.com
RURAL COMMUNITY
Brihuega (New Vraja Mandala) – (Santa Clara) 19411 Brihuega / Tel. +34 949 280436
RESTAURANT
Barcelona – Restaurante Govinda, Plaza de la Villa de Madrid 4–5, 08002/ Tel. +34 93 318-7729

SWEDEN

◆ **Gothenburg** – Karl Johansgatan 57, SE-414 55, Göteborg/ Tel. +46 (31) 421642/ info@harekrishnagoteborg.com
Grödinge – Radha-Krishna Temple, Korsnäs Gård, 14792 Grödinge/ Tel. +46 (8) 53029800/ Fax: +46 (8) 53025062/ bmd@pamho.net
◆ **Lund** – Bredgatan 28, 222 21/ Tel. +46 (46) 399500; Restaurant: +46 (46) 120413/ Fax: +46 (46) 188804/ locan@pamho.net
◆ **Stockholm** – Fridhemsgatan 22, 11240/ Tel. +46 (8) 654-9002/ Fax: +46 (8) 650-8813/ Restaurant: Tel. & fax: +46 (8) 654-9004/ lokanatha@hotmail.com
RURAL COMMUNITY
Järna – Almviks Gård, 153 95/ Tel. +46 (8551) 52050/ Fax: +46 (8551) 52060/ info@almviksgard.se
ADDITIONAL RESTAURANT
Malmo – Govinda's, Brogatan 11, 211 44 Malmo/ Tel. +46 (732) 306663

OTHER COUNTRIES

Amsterdam, The Netherlands – Van Hilligaertstraat 17, 1072 JX/ Tel. +31 (20) 675-1404 or -1694/ Fax: +31 (20) 675-1405/ amsterdam@pamho.net
Antwerp, Belgium – Amerikalei 184, 2000/ Tel. +32 (03) 237-0037/ antwerpen@pamho.net
◆ **Bratislava, Slovakia** – Druzstevna 22, Marianka, Bratislava 900 33/ Tel. +421 (903) 617031/ bratislava@pamho.net
Cakovec, Croatia – Radnicka 2, Svaska ves, 40000 Cakovec/ Tel. & fax: +385 (40) 334312
Copenhagen, Denmark – Skjulhoj Alle 44, 2720 Vanlose, Copenhagen/ Tel. +45 4828 6446/ Fax: +45 4828 7331/ iskcon.denmark@pamho.net
Helsinki, Finland – Ruoholahdenkatu 24 D (III krs) 00180/ Tel. +358 (9) 694-9879 or -9837/ harekrishna@harekrishna.fi
Karlovac, Croatia – Set. Dr. Franje Tudmana 5a, Karlovac 47000/ Tel. & fax: +385 (47) 600601/ info@avadhuta.hr
Kaunas, Lithuania – 37, Savanoryu pr., 3000/ Tel. +370 (7) 22-2574 or 26-8953/ Fax: +370 (7) 70-6642/ krsna.info@gmail.com
Kokosovce, Slovakia – Abranovce 60, 08252 Kokosovce/ Tel. +421 (51) 7798482
◆ **Lisbon, Portugal** – Rua Dona Estefania, 91 R/C 1000 Lisboa/ Tel. & fax: +351 (1) 314-0314 or 352-0038
◆ **Ljubljana, Slovenia** – Zibertova 27, 1000/ Tel. +386 (1) 4312319 or 4312124/ Fax: +386 (61) 310815/ ananta.rns@pamho.net
◆ **Locarno, Switzerland** – Govinda Rama, Via Borghese 14, 6600/ Tel. +41 (091) 752-3851/ Fax: +41 (091) 752-3852/ bhaktya.labhya.hks@pamho.net
Osijek, Croatia – Ivana Gundulica 9, 31000 Osijek/ Tel. +385 (31) 202759
Oslo, Norway – Roahagan 1D, Oslo 0754/ Tel. +47 (22) 062266/ gaurahari.sdha@pamho.net
Paris, France – 230 Avenue de la Division Leclerc, 95200 Sarcelles Village/ Tel. +33 (1) 39885358/ paris@pamho.net
Porto, Portugal – Rua S. Miguel 19, 4050-560 (mail: Apartado 4108, 4002-001)/ Tel. & fax: +351 (222) 007-223/ oriente.porto@teleweb.pt
Prague, Czech Republic – Jilova 290, Prague 5 - Zlicin 155 21/ Tel. +420 (2) 5795-0391/ info@harekrsna.cz
Pula, Croatia – Vinkuran centar 58, 52000 (mail: P.O. Box 16)/ Tel. & fax: +385 (52) 573581
◆ **Radhadesh, Belgium** – Chateau de Petite Somme, 6940 Septon-Durbuy/ Tel. +32 (086) 322926 (restaurant: 321421)/ Fax: +32 (086) 322929/ radhadesh@pamho.net
◆ **Riga, Latvia** – Krishyana Barona 56, Riga LV1011/ Tel. +371 67272490 or 29513891/ Fax: +371 67272491/ iskcon@balticom.lv
Rijeka, Croatia – Ivana Zajca 6/2, 51000 Rijeka (mail: P.O. Box 61)/ Tel. +385 (98) 697436/ info@harekrsna-ri.com
Sarajevo, Bosnia-Herzegovina – Prosorska 11, 71000/ Tel. +387 (33) 644 387/ templesarajevo@yahoo.com
Skopje, Macedonia – Centar za Vedski Studii, ul. Borka Taleski, br 43, 1000 Skopje/ Tel. +389 70371717/ vaideha@mt.net.mk
Sofia, Bulgaria – 4 J. Kjuri Str., 1113 Sofia/ Tel. +359 (2) 9719714/ iskcon@harekrishnabg.com
Sofia, Bulgaria – 119 Kliment Ohridski Str., kv. Malinova Dolina/ Tel. +359 (2) 9616050/ oks_sofia@abv.bg
◆ **Tallinn, Estonia** – Luise St. 11a, 10142/ Tel.

+372 6460047/ info@harekrishna.ee
Timisoara, Romania – Porumbescu 92, 1900/ Tel. & fax +40 (56) 154776
Vilnius, Lithuania – 23-1, Raugyklos G, 2024/ Tel. +370 (5) 2135218/ vilnius@pamho.net
Warsaw, Poland – Mysiadlo k. Warszawy, 05-500 Piaseczno, ul. Zakret 11/ Tel. +48 (22) 750-7797 or -8247/ Fax: +48 (22) 750-8249/ kryszna@post.pl
Wroclaw, Poland – ul. Brodzka 157, 54067 Wroclaw/ Tel. & fax: +48 (71) 354-3802/ nowenawadwip@gmail.com
Zagreb, Croatia – Centar Za Vedske Studije, II Bizet 36, 10000 (mail: P.O. Box 68, 10001)/ Tel. & fax: +385 (1) 3772-643/ ripuha@pamho.net
Zürich, Switzerland – Bergstrasse 54, 8032/ Tel. +41 (044) 262 33 88/ Fax: +41 (044) 262 31 14/ kgs@pamho.net

RURAL COMMUNITIES

Czech Republic – Krisnuv Dvur, Mestecko u Benesova, Postupice 257 01/ Tel. +420 (603) 700512 or 215380/ farma@krisnuvdvur.cz
France (La Nouvelle Mayapura) – Domaine d'Oublaisse, 36360, Lucay le Mâle/ Tel. +33 (2) 5440-2395/ Fax: +33 (2) 5440-2893/ oublaise@free.fr
Poland (New Santipur) – Czarnow 21, 58-424 Pisarzowice, woj. dolnoslaskie/ Tel. +48 (75) 744-8892/ radhu@wp.pl

ADDITIONAL RESTAURANTS

Bratislava, Slovakia – Govinda, Obchodna 30, 811 06 Bratislava/ Tel. +421 (2) 5926 2366
Kosice, Slovakia – Govinda, Puskinova 8, 040 01 Kosice/ Tel. +421 (910) 947112
Locarno, Switzerland – Govinda Restaurant, Via Della Motta 10, Locarno 6600/ Tel. +41 (091) 7523852 or 796260804/ radhakanta@pamho.net
Ljubljana, Slovenia – Holyfood (snackbar), Igriska 5, 1000 Ljubljana/ Tel. +386 (1) 251 13 84 or (41) 32 37 19
Oslo, Norway – Krishna's Cuisine, Kirkeveien 59B, 0364/ Tel. +47 (22) 606-250
Prague, Czech Republic – Govinda's, Soukenicka 27, 110 00 Prague 1/ Tel. +420 (2) 2481-6631 or 2481-6016/ info@harekrsna.cz
Prague, Czech Republic – Govinda's, Na hrazi 5, 180 00 Prague 8–Liben/ Tel. +420 (2) 8482-3805/ restaurace@govinda.cz
Prague, Czech Republic – Balarama, Orlicka 9, 130 00 Praha 3–Vinohrady/ Tel. +420 (2) 2272 8885/ info@balarama.cz
Presov, Slovakia – Govinda, Hlavna 70, 08001/ Tel. +421 (910) 947108
Tallinn, Estonia – Damodara, Lauteri St. 1, 10114/ Tel. +372 6442650

COMMONWEALTH OF INDEPENDENT STATES

RUSSIA

Astrahan – 141052, 8-59, Botvina St./ Tel. +7 (8512) 289431
Chita – 27, Kurnatovskogo St./ Tel. +7 (3022) 234971 or 230911
Ekaterinburg – 620078, G. Ekaterinburg, per. Otdelniy 5DK VOG/ Tel. +7 (343) 2742200 or 2595262
Irkutsk – St. Krimskaya 6A/ Tel. +7 (3952) 387132 or 324062/ irkutsk@cis.pamho.net
Kazan – 13, Sortirovochnaya St. pos.Yudino/ Tel. +7 (843) 2552529 or 2429991
Krasnodar – 418, Stepnaya St., selo Elizavetinskoye, Krsnodarski krai/ Tel. +7 (861) 2501694
Kurjinovo – 8, Shosseinaya St., pos. Ershovo, Urupski region, Karachayevo-Cherkessia
Moscow – Leningradsky Prospect, Vladenie 39 (mail: Begovaya str., 13, OPS 284, a/ya 17, 125284 Moscow)/
Tel. +7 (495) 7394377/ temple@veda.ru
Moscow – Sri Jagannath Mandir, Selskohozyaistvennaya St. 36, Building 1, Moscow 129323/ Tel. +7 (495) 6421084/ jaduradja@rambler.ru
Murmansk – 16, Frolova St. (mail: P.O. Box 5823)/ Tel. +7 (8152) 58-9284/ upendra@mun.rospac.ru
Nijny Novgorod – 14b, Chernigovskaya St., 603001/ Tel. +7 (8312) 305197 or 252592
Novorossijsk – 117, Shillerovskaya St./ Tel. +7 (8617) 438926 or 451415
Novosikirsk –18/2 Kholodilynaya St., 630001/ Tel. +7 (383) 2462655 or 2462666
Omsk – 664099, 42 10th Severnaya St. (mail: P.O. Box 8741)/ Tel. +7 (3812) 245310 or 2414051
Perm – 76, Generala Chernyakhovskogo, 614000/ Tel. +7 (342) 2755002 or 2260681/ prema.vardhana.das@cis.pamho.net
Rostov-Na-Donu – 84/1, Saryana St., 344025 (mail: P.O. Box 64, 344007)/ Tel. & fax: +7 (48636) 2510456
Samara – 122, Aeroportovskoye sh., Zubchininovka/ Tel. +7 (846) 2970318 or 2970323
Simbirsk – 10, Glinki St., 432002/ Tel. +7 (842) 2414016
Sochi – 81a, Lesnaya St., Bytha/ Tel. +7 (8622)

985639/ Tel. & fax: +7 (8622) 972483
Ulan-Ude – Prirechnaya St. 23, 670013 (mail: P.O. Box 4268, 670000)/ Tel. +7 (3012) 30795/ ulan.ude@cis.pamho.net
Vladimir – Ul. Nikolo-Galeyskaya 56/25, 60000/ Tel. +7 (4922) 326726
Vladivostok – Pikhtovaya St., 33/ Tel. +7 (4232) 35-30-26/ nram@list.ru

RESTAURANTS

Ekaterinburg – Sankirtana, 33 Bardina St./ Tel. +7 (343) 2412737
St. Petersburg – Govinda's, 58, Angliysky pr., 190008/ Tel. +7 (812) 1137896
Vladivostok – Vedic Cuisine, 12, Oleansky pr./ Tel. +7 (4232) 26-89-43/ nram@list.ru

UKRAINE

Dnipropetrovsk – Spusk Kalininskiy 39, 320038/ Tel. +380 (56) 2423631 or 2454709/ madan_gopal_psm@mail.ru
Donetsk – 22, Rubensa St., Makeyevka 339018/ Tel. +380 (62) 3491488/ premada@iskcon.donetsk.ua
Kharkov – 43, Verknegievskaya St., Holodnaya Gora, 310015/ Tel. +380 (57) 7242167/ kharkov@cis.pamho.net
Kiev – 21V, Dmitrievskaya ap.13, 01054/ Tel. +380 (44) 4844042 or 4821041/ Tel. & fax +380 (44) 4840934
Kiev – 16, Zoryany pereulok. 04078/ Tel. +380 (44) 4338312, or 4347028, or 4345533
Nikolaev – 5-8, Sudostroitelny per., 327052/ Tel. +380 (51) 2479422
Vinnica – 5, Chkalov St., 28601/ Tel. +380 (43) 2673171

OTHER COUNTRIES

Baku, Azerbaijan – 2A Sharili, Nizami Dist., AZ1002/ Tel. +994 (12) 4228376/ mammadov.azar@gmail.com
Bishkent, Kyrgyzstan – 5, Omsky per., 720007/ Tel. +996 (312) 242230
Dushanbe, Tajikistan – 38, Anzob St., 734001/ Tel. +7 (372) 271920 or 273990/ gurupriya@cada.tajik.net
Kishinev, Moldova – M. Cogalnichanu 59/ Tel. +373 (22) 277837
Minsk, Belarus – 11, Pavlova St., 220053/ Tel. +375 (17) 2880629/ new.jaipur@cis.pamho.net
Sukhumi, Georgia – St. Pr-t Mira d 274/ Tel. +995 (122) 29954
Tashkent, Uzbekistan – 54, A. Kodirov St., Mirabad Tumani, 700005/ Tel. & fax: +998 (371) 2918501/ tashkentmandir@mail.ru
Tbilisi, Georgia – 16, Kacharava St., Avchalskoye sh., 380053/ Tel. +995 (32) 623326 or 985812

RESTAURANT

Almaty, Kazakhstan – Govinda's, 39 Ablay Khan Ave., Almaty City 050004/ Tel. +7 (727) 2710836/ Fax: +7 (327) 2713235/ kazakh@pamho.net

AUSTRALASIA

AUSTRALIA

Adelaide – 25 Le Hunte St. (mail: P.O. Box 114, Kilburn, SA 5084)/ Tel. +61 (8) 8359-5120/ iskconsa@tpg.com.au
Brisbane – 95 Bank Rd., Graceville (mail: P.O. Box 83, Indooroopilly), QLD 4068/ Tel. +61 (7) 3379-5455/
Canberra – 44 Limestone Ave., Ainslie, ACT 2602 (mail: P.O. Box 1411, Canberra, ACT 2601)/ Tel. +61 (2) 6262-6208/
Melbourne – 197 Danks St. (mail: P.O. Box 125), Albert Park, VIC 3206/ Tel. +61 (3) 9699-5122/ melbourne@pamho.net
Perth – 155-159 Canning Rd., Kalamunda (mail: P.O. Box 201 Kalamunda 6076)/ Tel. +61 (8) 6293-1519/ perth@pamho.net
Sydney – 180 Falcon St., North Sydney, NSW 2060 (mail: P.O. Box 459, Cammeray, NSW 2062)/ Tel. +61 (2) 9959-4558/ admin@iskcon.com.au
Sydney – Govinda's Yoga & Meditation Centre, 112 Darlinghurst Rd., Darlinghurst NSW 2010 (mail: P.O. Box 174, Kings Cross 1340)/ Tel. +61 (2) 9380-5162/ sita@govindas.com.au

RURAL COMMUNITIES

Bambra, VIC (New Nandagram) – 50 Seaches Outlet, off 1265 Winchelsea Deans Marsh Rd., Bambra VIC 3241/ Tel. +61 (3) 5288-7383
Cessnock, NSW (New Gokula) – Lewis Lane, off Mount View Road, Millfield, near Cessnock (mail: P.O. Box 399, Cessnock, NSW 2325)/ Tel. +61 (2) 4998-1800/ Fax: iskconfarm@mac.com
Murwillumbah, NSW (New Govardhana) – Tyalgum Rd., Eungella (mail: P.O. Box 687), NSW 2484/ Tel. +61 (2) 6672-6579/ Fax: +61 (2) 6672-5498/ ajita@in.com.au

RESTAURANTS

Brisbane – Govinda's, 99 Elizabeth St., 1st Floor, QLD 4000/ Tel. +61 (7) 3210-0255
Brisbane – Krishna's Cafe, 1st Floor, 82 Vulture St., West End, QLD 4000/ Tel. +61 (7) 3844-2316/ brisbane@pamho.net
Burleigh Heads – Govinda's, 20 James St., Burleigh Heads, QLD 4220/ Tel. +61 (7) 5607-0782/ ajita@in.com.au

Maroochydore — Govinda's Vegetarian Cafe, 2/7 First Ave., QLD 4558/ Tel. +61 (7) 5451-0299
Melbourne — Crossways, 1st Floor, 123 Swanston St., VIC 3000/ Tel. +61 (3) 9650-2939
Melbourne — Gopal's, 139 Swanston St., VIC 3000/ Tel. +61 (3) 9650-1578
Perth — Govinda's Restaurant, 194 William St., Northbridge, W.A. 6003/ Tel. +61 (8) 9227-1684/ perth@pamho.net

NEW ZEALAND AND FIJI

Auckland, NZ — The Loft, 1st Floor, 103 Beach Rd./ Tel. +64 (9) 3797301
Christchurch, NZ — 83 Bealey Ave. (mail: P.O. Box 25-190)/ Tel. +64 (3) 366-5174/ iskconchch@clear.net.nz
Hamilton, NZ — 188 Maui St., RD 8, Te Rapa/ Tel. +64 (7) 850-5108/ rmaster@wave.co.nz
Labasa, Fiji — Delailabasa (mail: P.O. Box 133)/ Tel. +679 812912
Lautoka, Fiji — 5 Tavewa Ave. (mail: P.O. Box 125)/ Tel. +679 666 4112/ regprakash@excite.com
Nausori, Fiji — Hare Krishna Cultural Centre, 2nd Floor, Shop & Save Building, 11 Gulam Nadi St., Nausori Town (mail: P.O. Box 2183, Govt. Bldgs., Suva)/ Tel. +679 996 9748 or 347 5097/ vdas@frca.org.fj
Rakiraki, Fiji — Rewasa (mail: P.O. Box 204)/ Tel. +679 694243
Sigatoka, Fiji — Queens Rd., Olosara (mail: P.O. Box 1020)/ Tel. +679 9373703 or 6520866/ drgsmarna@connect.com.fj
Suva, Fiji — 166 Brewster St. (mail: P.O. Box 4229, Samabula)/ Tel. +679 331 8441/ iskconsuva@connect.com.fj
Wellington, NZ — 105 Newlands Rd., Newlands/ Tel. +64 (4) 478-4108/ info@iskconwellington.org.nz
Wellington, NZ — Gaura Yoga Centre, 1st Floor, 175 Vivian St. (mail: P.O. Box 6271, Marion Square)/ Tel. +64 (4) 801-5500/ yoga@gaurayoga.co.nz

RURAL COMMUNITY

Auckland, NZ (New Varshan) — Hwy. 28, Riverhead, next to Huapai Golf Course (mail: R.D. 2, Kumeu)/ Tel. +64 (9) 412-8075

RESTAURANTS

Auckland, NZ — Hare Krishna Food for Life, 268 Karangahape Rd./ Tel. +64 (9) 300-7585
Labasa, Fiji — Hare Krishna Restaurant, Naseakula Road/ Tel. +679 811364
Lautoka, Fiji — Gopal's, Corner of Yasawa Street and Naviti Street/ Tel. +679 662990
Suva, Fiji — Hare Krishna Vegetarian Restaurant, Dolphins FNPF Place, Victoria Parade/ Tel. +679 314154/ vdas@govnet.gov.fj
Suva, Fiji — Hare Krishna Vegetarian Restaurant, Opposite University of the South Pacific, Laucala Bay Rd./ Tel. +679 311683/ vdas@govnet.gov.fj
Suva, Fiji — Hare Krishna Vegetarian Restaurant, 18 Pratt St./ Tel. +679 314154
Suva, Fiji — Hare Krishna Vegetarian Restaurant, 82 Ratu Mara Rd., Samabula/ Tel. +679 386333
Suva, Fiji — Hare Krishna Vegetarian Restaurant, Terry Walk, Cumming St./ Tel. +679 312295
Wellington, NZ — Higher Taste Hare Krishna Restaurant, Old Bank Arcade, Ground Flr., Corner Customhouse, Quay & Hunter St., Wellington/ Tel. +64 (4) 472-2233/ Fax: (4) 472-2234/ highertaste@iskconwellington.org.nz

AFRICA

GHANA

Accra — Samsam Rd., Off Accra-Nsawam Hwy., Medie, Accra North (mail: P.O. Box 11686)/ Tel. & fax +233 (21) 229988/ srivas_bts@yahoo.co.in
Kumasi — Twumduasi, near Boadi-Emina, off Kumasi-Accra Road, 3 km from Aninwaa Hospital, Emina, Kumasi/ Tel +233 208320816/ gaurangainkumasi@gmail.com
Nkawkaw — P.O. Box 69
Sunyani — Plot No. 146, South Ridge Estates (mail P.O. Box 685)
Takoradi — New Amanful, P.O. Box 328
Tarkwa — State Housing Estate, Cyanide

RURAL COMMUNITIES

Agona Swedru — Hare Krishna Village, Off Swedru-Winneba Highway, Agona Swedru, Central Region (mail: P.O. Box SW 953, Agonu Swedru 00233)/ Tel. +233 249969922 or 208318312/ harekrishnavillage@in.com
Eastern Region — Hare Krishna Farm Community, P.O. Box 15, Old Akrade

NIGERIA

Abeokuta — Ibadan Rd., Obanatoka (mail: P.O. Box 5177)
Benin City — 108, Lagos-Uselu Rd., Uselu/ Tel. +234 (52) 258636, +234 8023524924, or +234 8056283995/ acharyapurandara2000@yahoo.com
Enugu — 5/6, Destiny Layout, Old Abakaliki Rd., Near Enugu Airport, Emene (by Efemelumna Bus Stop)/ Tel. +234 8035822545
Ibadan — 700 meters from Iwo Rd., Ibadan-Lagos Express Way, University of Ibadan (mail: P.O. Box 9996)/ Tel. +234 8034687595/ salika108@hotmail.com
Jos — Gwarandok Rd., Near Air Force Base,

Abattoir Rd., by Nammua, Giring Village (mail: P.O. Box 6557)/ Tel. +234 8034711933/ salika108@hotmail.com
Kaduna — Federal Housing Estate, Abuja Rd., Goningora Village (mail: P.O. Box 1121)/ Tel. +234 8035405080/ atreyarishi@yahoo.com
Lagos — No. 23 Egbeyemi St., Off Coker Rd., Illupeju, Lagos (mail: P.O. Box 8793, Marina)/ Tel. +234 8069245577 or 7066011800/ iskconlagos@yahoo.com
Port Harcourt — Umuebule 11, 2nd tarred road, Etche (mail: P.O. Box 4429, Trans Amadi)/ Tel. +234 8033215096/ canakyus@yahoo.com
Warri — Okwodiete Village, Kilo 8, Effurun/ Orerokpe Rd. (mail: P.O. Box 1922)/ Tel. +234 8033451265/ kamalaksa@yahoo.com

SOUTH AFRICA

Cape Town — 17 St. Andrews Rd., Rondebosch 7700/ Tel. +27 (21) 6861179/ Fax: +27 (21) 686-8233/ cape.town@pamho.net
◆ **Durban** — 50 Bhaktivedanta Swami Circle, Unit 5 (mail: P.O. Box 56003), Chatsworth, 4030/ Tel. +27 (31) 403-3328/ Fax: +27 (31) 403-4429/ iskcon.durban@pamho.net
Johannesburg — 7971 Capricorn Ave. (entrance on Nirvana Drive East), Ext. 9, Lenasia (mail: P.O. Box 926, Lenasia 1820)/ Tel. +27 (11) 854-1975 or -7969/ iskconjh@iafrica.com
Phoenix — 72 Pandora St., Phoenix 4068 (mail: P.O. Box 60992, Phoenix 4060)/ Tel. +27 (31) 507-6559/ Fax: (031) 500-1923/ iskcon.phoenix@pamho.net
Pretoria — 1189 Church St., Hatfield 0083 (mail: P.O. Box 14077, Hatfield 0028)/ Tel. & fax: +27 (12) 342-6216/ iskcon.pretoria@pamho.net

OTHER COUNTRIES

Abidjan, Cote D'Ivoire — Temple Hare Krishna (AICK-CI), Cocody-Angre, Cite Blanche, Villa 238/ Tel. +225 22423980, 05648329 or 08416770/ carudesnabts@yahoo.fr
Baie du Cap, Mauritius — St. Martin/ Tel. +230 521-0028
Gaboronne, Botswana — P.O. Box 201003/ Tel. +267 3307768/ Fax: +267 3301988/ dkkoshal@infow.bw
Kampala, Uganda — 9 Dewington Rd. (mail: P.O. Box 1647), Kampala/ Tel. +256 7564-2741
Kisumu, Kenya — Cairo Rd., P.O. Box 9202/ Tel. +254 (57) 40983/ Fax: +254 (57) 43827
◆ **Lome, Togo** — Sis Face Place Bonke, Cote Blue Night, Tokoin Hospital, 01 BP 3105/ Tel. + 228 2217477 or 9028793/ varaha.bts@pamho.net
Marondera, Zimbabwe — 6 Pine Street (mail: P.O. Box 339)/ Tel. +263 (28) 887-7801
Mombasa, Kenya — Hare Krishna House, Sauti Ya Kenya and Kisumu Rds. (mail: P.O. Box 82224)/ Tel. +254 (41) 312248
Nairobi, Kenya — Hare Krishna Close, Off West Nagara Rd., Nairobi 0100 (mail: P.O. Box 28946)/ Tel. +254 (20) 3744365/ Fax: +254 (20) 3740957/ iskcon_nairobi@yahoo.com
◆ **Phoenix, Mauritius** — 72 Pandora St., Phoenix 4068 (mail: P.O. Box 60992, Phoenix 4060)/ Tel. +230 507-6559/ Fax: +230 500-1923
Rose Belle, Mauritius —Shivala Lane/ Tel. +230 627-5030

RURAL COMMUNITIES

Mauritius (ISKCON Vedic Farm) — Hare Krishna Rd., Vrindaban/ Tel. +230 418-3185 or 418-3955/ Fax: +230 418-6470
Uganda (Hare Krishna Farm) — Seeta Town, Kampala

LATIN AMERICA

ARGENTINA

Buenos Aires — Centro Bhaktivedanta, Andonaegui 2054, Villa Urquiza, CP 1431/ Tel. +54 (11) 523-4232/ Fax: +54 (11) 523-8085/ iskcon-ba@gopalnet.com
Rosario — Paraguay 556 (2000)/ Tel. +54 (341) 252630 or 264243/ Fax: +54 (341) 490838
San Miguel — Muqoz 1745, entre Concejal Tribulato y Espaqa, (1663), Pcia. Buenos Aires/ Tel. +54 (11) 4664-6631 or 4667-0483/ bhaktiyoga@sinectis.com.ar

RURAL COMMUNITY

Bhaktilata Puri — Ciudad de la Paz 3554 (1429) Capital Federal/ Tel. & fax: +54 (11) 523-8085

RESTAURANTS

Buenos Aires — Jagannath Prasadam, Triunvirato 4266 (1431)/ Tel. +54 (11) 521-3396
Buenos Aires — Restaurante Tulasi, Marcelo T. de Alvear 628, Local 30

BOLIVIA

Cochabamba — Villa Vaikuntha, Av. Ayacucho entre cale La Paz y Tte. Arevalo # 108/ Tel. +591 70610864/ villa.vaikuntha.bo@gmail.com
◆ **Santa Cruz** — Calle 27 de Mayo No. 99 esq. Justo Bazan/ Tel. & fax: +591 (3) 345189

RURAL COMMUNITY

Bolivia — (contact ISKCON Cochabamba)

RESTAURANTS

Cochabamba — Restaurant Gopal, calle España N-250 (Galeria Olimpia)/ Tel. +591 (4) 234082
Cochabamba — Restaurant Govinda, calle Mexico #E0303/ Tel. +591 (4) 222568

Cochabamba — Restaurant Tulasi, Av. Heroinas E-262
Oruro — Restaurant Govinda, Calle 6 de Octubre No. 6071
Santa Cruz — Snack Govinda, Calle Bolivar esq. Av. Argomosa (primer anillo)/ Tel. +591 (3) 345189
Sucre — Restaurant Sat Sanga, Calle Tarapacá No. 161/ Tel. +591 (64) 22547

BRAZIL

Belo Horizonte, MG — Rua Ametista, 212, Prado, 30410-420/ Tel. +55 (31) 3337-7645
◆ **Curitiba, PR** — Rua Panamá, Bairro Bacacheri, Curitiba 82510-170/ Tel. +55 (41) 3015-5106/ iskconctba@yahoo.com.br
◆ **Porto Alegre, RS** — Rua Jose Bonifacio, 605, Bom Fim, 90040-130/ Tel. +55 (51) 3332-1704/ mail@harekrishnapoa.org.br
◆ **Recife, PE** — Rua Bernardo Guimaraes, 114, Boa Vista, 50050-440/ Tel. +55 (32) 214-2021/ nitaygouranga@ig.com.br
Rio de Janeiro, RJ — Estrada da Barra da Tijuca, 1990, Itanhangá, Rio de Janeiro, RJ/ Tel. +55 (21) 3563-1627/ contato@harekrishnarj.com.br
Salvador, BA — Rua Alvaro Adorno, 17, Brotas, 40255-460/ salvador@iskconbahia.com.br
Sao Paulo, SP — Rua Tomas Goncalves 70, Butanta, 05590-030/ Tel. +55 (11) 8496-3158/ comunicacao@harekrishnasp.com.br
Suzano, SP — Rua XV, 585, Jardim Gardenia, 08696-550/ Tel. +55 (11) 4752-2553/ info@suzanomandir.com.br

RURAL COMMUNITIES

Caruaru, PE (Nova Vrajadhama) — Serra dos Cavalos, Distrito de Murici, P.O. Box 283, 55000-000/ yagnivi@yahoo.com.br
Parati, RJ (Goura Vrindavana) — P.O. Box 74.862, 23970-000/ Tel. +55 (24) 3371-7364/ goura@paratyweb.com.br
◆ **Pindamonhangaba, SP (Nova Gokula)** — Ribeirao Grande, P.O. Box 1009, 12400-990/ Tel. +55 (12) 3645-8238/ giriraj@ig.com.br
Teresopolis, RJ (Vrajabhumi) — Prata dos Aredes, P.O. Box 92430, 25953-970/Tel. +55 (21) 2644-7213/ lrvraja@uol.com.br

ADDITIONAL RESTAURANTS

Campina Grande, PB — Govinda, Rua Teodosio de Oliveira Ledo, 144, Centro, 58101-440/ Tel. +55 (83) 342-0239/ mahanm12000@yahoo.com.br
Curitiba, PR — ISKCON Restaurant, R. Paula Gomes, 123, Proximo Shopping Muller, Curitiba 80510-070/ Tel. +55 (41) 3024-5225
Sao Paulo, SP — Gopala Prasada, Rua Antonio Carlos, 413, 01309-011/ Tel. +55 (11) 3283-3867/ gopalaprasada@bol.com.br

MEXICO

◆ **Guadalajara** — Pedro Moreno No. 1791, Sector Juarez, Jalisco, 261278/ Tel. +52 (33) 616-4481
Mexico City — Tiburcio Montiel 45, Colonia San Miguel, Chapultepec D.F., 11850/ Tel. +52 (55) 5273-1953/ Fax: +52 (55) 5272-5944/ sugerencias@harekrishnamexico.com
Monterrey — Juan Ignacio Ramón 841, Col. Barrio Antiguo, entre Dr. Coss y Diego de Montemayor, Zona Centro, Nuevo León, 64000/ Tel. +52 (81) 8340-5950
Monterrey — Playa Revolcadero 3329, Col. Primavera, c.p. 64830/ Tel. +52 (81) 8387-1883/ ambujaksa.gps@pamho.net
Saltillo — Blvd. Saltillo No. 520, Col. Buenos Aires/ Tel. +52 (844) 417-8752/ ramayana@todito.com

RURAL COMMUNITY

Guadalajara — (contact ISKCON Guadalajara)

ADDITIONAL RESTAURANTS

León Guanajuato — Radha Govinda Rest., Rusto Sierra 343, Centro, CP 37000/ Tel. +52 (477) 716-2280
Veracruz — Restaurante Radhe, Sur 5 No. 50, Orizaba, Ver./ Tel. +52 (2717) 14825

PERU

Lima — Pasaje Solea 101, Santa Maria-Chosica/ Tel. +51 (1) 360-3381
◆ **Lima** — Schell 634 Miraflores/ Tel. +51 (1) 444-2871
◆ **Lima** — Av. Garcilaso de la Vega 1670/ Tel. +51 (1) 433-2589

RURAL COMMUNITY

Correo De Bella Vista — DPTO De San Martin

ADDITIONAL RESTAURANT

Cuzco — Espaderos 128

OTHER COUNTRIES

Asunción, Paraguay — Centro Bhaktivedanta, Mariano R. Alonso 925/ Tel. +595 (21) 480-266/ Fax: +595 (21) 490-449
Caracas, Venezuela — Av. Los Proceres (con Calle Marquez del Toro), San Bernardino/ Tel. +58 (212) 550-1818
Essequibo Coast, Guyana — New Navadvipa Dham, Mainstay, Essequibo Coast/ Tel. +592 771-4894
Guayaquil, Ecuador — 6 de Marzo 226 and V. M. Rendon/ Tel. +593 (4) 308412 or 309420/ Fax: +593 (4) 302108/ gurumani@gu.pro.ec
Panama, Republic of Panama — Via las

Cumbres, entrada Villa Zaita, casa #10, frente a INPSA, (mail: P.O. Box 6-1776, El Dorado)/ Tel. +507 231-6561/ iskconpanama@hotmail.com
Paramaribo, Suriname — Kwattaweg #459 (mail: P.O. Box 713)/ Tel. & fax: +597 435051/ Tel. +597 8541988/ iskcon.suriname@pamho.net
Pereira, Colombia — Carrera 5a, No.19-36
San Jose, Costa Rica — Barrio Roosvelt en San Pedro, dos cuadras al sur del Mall Outlet, diagonal a la plaza de futbol, casa esquinera/ Tel. +506 2524-1196 or 2537-4216/ iskcon-costarica@hotmail.com
San Salvador, El Salvador — 8a Avenida Norte, Casa No. 2–4, Santa Tecla, La Libertad/ Tel. +503 2288-2900/ mail@harekrishnaelsalvador.com
Santiago, Chile — Carrera 330/ Tel. +56 (2) 698-8044/ adikesavadasa@yahoo.com.ar
Santo Domingo, Dominican Republic — Calle San Francisco de Asis No. 73, Ensanche Ozama/ Tel. +1 (809) 597-5078/ svats1949@hotmail.com
Trinidad and Tobago, West Indies — Eastern Main Rd., Garden Village, Arouca (mail: B. Narine, Rice Mill Rd., Garden Village, Arouca)/ Tel. +1 (868) 646-1062
Trinidad & Tobago, West Indies — 4 Orion Dr., Debe/ Tel. +1 (868) 647-6809/ iskcondebe@yahoo.com
Trinidad & Tobago, West Indies — Edinburgh Rd., Longdenville, Chaguanas/ Tel. +1 (868) 665-2249/ agni.sdg@pamho.net
West Coast Demerara, Guyana — Sri Gaura Nitai Ashirvad Mandir, Lot "B," Nauville Flanders (Crane Old Road), West Coast Demerara/ Tel. +592 254 0494/ iskcon.guyana@yahoo.com
West Coast Demerara, Guyana — New Godruma, 24 Uitvlugt Front, West Coast Demerara
Williamsburg, Guyana — New Kulinagram, Block 6, Williamsburg, Corentyne, Berbice/ Tel. +592 333-3563/ prabhoh@yahoo.com

RURAL COMMUNITIES

Colombia (Nueva Mathura) — Cruzero del Guali, Municipio de Caloto, Valle del Cauca/ Tel. +57 (2) 361-2688
Costa Rica (Nueva Goloka Vrindavana) — Carretera Cartago-Paraiso, de la iglesia cristiana Rios de Agua Viva, 75 metros al oeste y 300 metros al sudeste, Cartago (mail: Apartado 166, 1002, San Jose)/ Tel. +506 551-0990/ prthvipavana@yahoo.com
Ecuador (Giridhari Desa) — Chordeleg km 5, Via Sig-sig, Cuenca/ Tel. +593 (7) 2887599 or 2830462/ jervesmr@etapa.com.ec
Ecuador (Nueva Mayapur) — Ayampe (near Guayaquil)
El Salvador — Carretera a Santa Ana, Km. 34, Canton Los Indios, Zapotitan, Dpto. de La Libertad
Trinidad (New Madhuvan) — Sri Jagannatha Mandir, mm #13 Cumuto Main Rd., Coryal/ Tel. +1 (868) 745-0294

This is a partial list.
Far from a center?
Call us at 1-800-927-4152.
Or contact us on the Internet.

http://www.krishna.com • E-mail: bbt.usa@krishna.com

The Nectar of Devotion

(Offer valid in US only.)

Take advantage of this special offer and purchase *The Nectar of Devotion: The Complete Science of Bhakti Yoga,* for only **$9.75**. This is a savings of **25% off** the regular price. To receive this discount you must mention the following code when you place your order: NOD-ISO.

ORDER TOLL FREE 1-800-927-4152

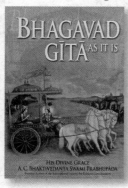

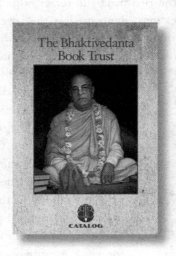